Her perseverance and faith have inspired millions worldwide and made her the subject of a major motion picture.

Now, nearly a decade after she lost her arm in a shark attack at the age of thirteen, professional surfer Bethany Hamilton's incredible story reverberates with hope and one universal truth: Anything is possible if you trust in God and yourself.

PRAISE FOR *SOUL SURFER*

"Hamilton's optimism, determination, and resilience are undeniably impressive and uplifting."

—*Publishers Weekly*

"Hamilton's account is suffused with her feelings for God and His impact on her life. Perhaps because of this relationship, she never seems depressed about her situation. . . . [The book] has automatic appeal for a wide range of readers."

—*Booklist*

This title is also available as an eBook.

soul surfer

A True Story of Faith, Family, and Fighting to Get Back on the Board

Bethany Hamilton

With Sheryl Berk and Rick Bundschuh

POCKET
BOOKS

MTV BOOKS

NEW YORK   LONDON   TORONTO   SYDNEY   NEW DELHI

Dedicated to

Jesus Christ, my family

and the Blanchard family.

Pocket Books
A Division of Simon & Schuster, Inc.
1230 Avenue of the Americas
New York, NY 10020

Copyright © 2004, 2011 by Bethany Hamilton

MTV Music Television and all related titles, logos, and characters are trademarks of MTV Networks, a division of Viacom International Inc.

All photos courtesy of Noah Hamilton and the Hamilton family.

All rights reserved, including the right to reproduce this book or portions thereof in any form whatsoever. For information address Pocket Books Subsidiary Rights Department, 1230 Avenue of the Americas, New York, NY 10020

This MTV Books/Pocket Books paperback edition July 2012

POCKET and colophon are registered trademarks of Simon & Schuster, Inc.

For information about special discounts for bulk purchases, please contact Simon & Schuster Special Sales at 1-866-506-1949 or business@simonandschuster.com.

The Simon & Schuster Speakers Bureau can bring authors to your live event. For more information or to book an event contact the Simon & Schuster Speakers Bureau at 1-866-248-3049 or visit our website at www.simonspeakers.com

Manufactured in the United States of America

10   9   8   7   6   5

ISBN 978-1-4516-7913-7
ISBN 978-1-4165-1084-0 (ebook)

acknowledgments

My family and I would like to acknowledge and thank all the people that have helped and supported me through this difficult and challenging period in my life. I am grateful for every single person God has put in my life and I thank Him for each and every one of you. Another book could be written just to thank all the people who have sent their love and support. I have been blessed and I know this is to help me grow and be strong so I can be a blessing to others. I want to acknowledge and thank God for his unconditional love that He has for everyone and for the wonderful friends and family He has given me.

Holt, Cydney, Byron, Alana, and Dorian Blanchard; Roy, Tiffany, Chantilly, and Dutch Hofstetter; Andy, Jill, Alex, Travis, and Koa Smith; Sheryl Berk and her beautiful daughter Carrie; Louise Burke, Liate Stehlik, Hillary Schupf, Lauren McKenna and the team at Pocket Books; Jacob Hoye and the team at MTV Books; Eric Kusky, Ken Raasch and the team at Creative Brands Group; World Vision Foundation; Al Burton, Rob Heddon, and the Hollywood Scene; Emily Just and the ABC family; The Inside Edition Team; Pastor Steve and Trish Thompson; Troy and Malia Gall; Sarah Hill, Wayne Cordeiro and New Hope Christian Fellowship, Oahu; North Shore Community Church Members; Rick Bundschuh and Kauai Christian Fellowship; Delta Breeze Church; Everyone involved in the Friends of Bethany Hamilton fundraiser; Charlie, Felicia Cowden and Hanalei Surf Co. Staff; Kauai lifeguards; Bill, Ronda, Laird, and Lyon Hamilton; Phil, Daniel, Andy, and Bruce Irons; Nelson Togioka; Ralph Young; Chris and Evelyn Cook;

Steve Jepson; Kim and Dave Dornbuch; Don and Barbara Toftee; Edwin Nakakura; Rick, Amy, Marvin and family; Patrice Pendaruis; Karen Mendoza; Becky and Baumgartner family; Schneider family; Coach Dick Oliver; Lani Yukimura and all the staff at the Wilcox Hospital that helped me; Dr. Dave Rovinsky; Dr. Ken Pierce; Dr. Richard Davis; Dr. Patrick Turley; Dr. Kai Swaggart; Dennis Fujimoto; Mike Coots; Joey Barca; Tim, Drema, Nate, Noelle Carroll; Steve and Nancy Cranston; Bobby and Miko Parker; Ben Aipa; Butch and Cammie Irving; Mike Latronic; Betty Depolito; Rabbit Kekai; Russell Lewis; Mike Neal and family; Chris Moore; Grandpa Jack; Grandma Dot; Debbie and Wayne Choate; Karin Lynch and family; Devon Geis and family; Craig and Tonci Hoshide; Monk and Cathy Monroe; Mike and Terry Perkins; all of the Hamilton family; all of the Gazsi family; John and Patty Crown and family; Shannon Kay; Rick and Jane Rosaler; Kathy and Denny; Rork Peca; Joey Buran; Kathy Koerner; Joe Thompson; Jeff

Denholm; Ellen Henderson; LeeAnn Sanders; Shoshana; Bridgeman family; Mock family; Danny Lehman; Bender family ; Bob Sato; Alikai and Titus Kinimaka; Grandma Mary Hamilton; Malemed family; Troy Farnsworth and Randy Alley—Hanger Inc.; Challenged Athletes Foundation; Australian Grand Prix; Steamboat Springs Ski Resort; Barry Zito and the Oakland A's; Chuck Smith and Calvary Chapel; North Shore Christian Church, Oahu; Alana, Carrissa and all the competitors that push me to be a better surfer; my sponsors: Rip Curl—Pod, Adam, Mike, and P.J.; Hanalei Surf Co.; Sticky Bumps—John, Chris and Dahl; Tim Carroll—Surfboards; Surf One—Skateboards Surf Co., Hawaii.

P.S. All my friends—sorry to those who were missed, thank you.

contents

foreword

To be honest, I never wanted to write a book.

It actually took a lot of convincing by my family and friends, because I'm not someone who likes to talk a lot about myself, or thinks I'm any big deal. But they saw something in my story that would be helpful and interesting to others—and they encouraged me to write it down. So here I am. And actually, when I *really* thought about it, it seemed like something that I should do. It would give a bigger picture of my faith, my family, and all those people who have helped get me back into the water again. But I'll tell you one thing: it wasn't easy.

It took a lot of people to help me put my thoughts on paper. First, there was Rick Bundschuh, my spiritual advisor and a pastor in the Kauai Christian Fellowship Church. There were certain things I just didn't want to talk about— certainly not to a stranger. So Rick volunteered to do the "translating." We would sit for hours and just talk, talk, talk. I'd pour my heart out, and he'd patiently listen, putting it all down on paper. Then came our writer, Sheryl Berk, who helped me organize and shape all these thoughts into fifteen chapters (who knew I had 200-plus pages in me?). When you're really close to something, it's hard to see things as they truly were or are. So Sheryl, along with my editor, Lauren McKenna, helped me connect the dots. They asked the toughest questions! Stuff that really made me squirm some-times, but also, in the end, made me dig a little deeper and really be honest with myself and you. In the end, I'm really proud of what we've written here. I think it's truthful, and I hope it inspires and motivates people to tackle any obstacles in their lives. I hope it helps people find faith in God and in their own strength and ability. I hope it motivates someone going through a tough time right now to keep on fighting until they rise above it. You can and will get through it. I'm living proof that where there's a will, there's a way.

What I don't want is for people to pity me or think of me as a person who has had her life ruined. That's not how I see it. My mom is always saying, "If life hands you lemons, make lemonade." Which is a great outlook on life, if you can actually see beyond the lemons when you're up to your eyeballs in them! My strength came from my relationship with Christ and from the love and encouragement of my family and friends.

In a lot of ways I'm like any fourteen-year-old girl, and in a lot of ways, I'm not. If someone had told me that this is how my life would be, I would have never believed it. It would have seemed too bizarre to be true. Sometimes it still is. I often dream that I have both my arms again, and I wake up expecting the whole shark business to be a nightmare. But it's not. It's my reality now, and I've learned to accept it. I've moved on.

I don't pretend to have all the answers to why bad things happen to good people. But I do know that God knows all those answers, and sometimes He lets you know in this life, and sometimes He asks you to wait so that you can have a face-to-face talk about it. What I do know is that I want to use what happened to me as an opportunity to tell people that God is worthy of our trust, and to show them that you can go on and do wonderful things in spite of terrible events that happen. I don't think it does any good to sit around feeling sorry for yourself. I made myself a promise: I'm not going to wallow or walk around moaning, "Woe is me!"

One other thing you should know: this book really doesn't have an ending yet because I am still learning how to cope every day. I'm not talking about learning how to button my top with one hand. I'm talking about coping with being a celebrity, something I never imagined that I would have to deal with at the age of fourteen. Or coping with people's stares, either because they recognize me, or because they are not used to seeing a person with one arm running down the beach. Or coping with answering endless questions from the media and seeing my face in newspapers and magazines. I'm also learning to cope with the frustration of knowing that if I had both arms to paddle, I just might have done a little better in a surf contest that I have just been in.

I am excited about some of the opportunities to travel and surf all around the world that have come as a result of my attack and return to surfing. But most of all I am excited about what the future holds. Will I make it to the pro ranks in surfing? Will my lifelong friend and surf buddy, Alana, be paddling next to me in the years to come as she is now and was during the attack? Will I be able to make a difference, in some small way, in people's lives by sharing my story?

What does God have in store for me? I really don't know, but I do know one thing for sure: the adventure has only started.

halloween morning

It came, literally, out of the blue.

I had no warning at all; not even the slightest hint of danger on the horizon. The water was crystal clear and calm; it was more like swimming in a pool, rather than the deep ocean waters in Kauai, Hawaii, where I go almost every morning to surf with my friend Alana Blanchard or the other girls on the Hanalei girls' surf team. The waves were small and inconsistent, and I was just kind of rolling along with them, relaxing on my board with my right hand on the nose of the board and my left arm dangling in the cool water. I remember thinking, "I hope the surf picks up soon . . . ," when suddenly there was a flash of gray.

That's all it took: a split second. I felt a lot of

pressure and a couple of lightning-fast tugs. I couldn't make out any of the details, but I knew that the huge jaws of a fifteen-foot tiger shark covered the top of my board and my left arm. Then I watched in shock as the water around me turned bright red. Somehow, I stayed calm and started to paddle toward the beach. My left arm was gone almost to the armpit, along with a huge, crescent-shaped chunk of my red-white-and-blue surfboard . . .

a morning like any other

It was still dark, about 5 A.M., when my mom, Cheri, cracked open my bedroom door, peeked inside, and called, "Wanna go surfing?" Before I had a chance to even open my eyes, our shar-pei, Ginger, jumped on my bed with her own wet good morning kiss. It was my usual surfing wakeup call.

I was hoping for a perfect surfing morning. It had poured for the last three days, but I couldn't hear the sound of the rain plopping on the big elephant-ear plants outside my window. *Yes!* Perhaps the storm had passed, and the warm tropical sunshine would be back today.

I lay there in bed a few minutes more, listening to my mom start her morning ritual: first, she flicks on the living room television and switches to the local island weather channel for the report while she brews a strong cup of coffee. She listens very carefully, not just to the forecast but also to the buoy reports that tell of swell activity. Then she translates all that info into a plan for me: she plots out where the best surf will likely be hitting the island.

I reached over to the nightstand and turned on the lamp switch. My lamp is pretty cool: it has a clear base that I filled with shells. In fact, my whole room is full of shells. I have a blue shell bedspread, shell necklaces, and boxes overflowing with my shell collection. I was once asked what I would grab if my room was on fire. No contest: I have lots of cool knickknacks, and dozens of trophies from winning amateur surf contests, but I am sure the first thing I would grab would be my beautiful sunrise shells. (Their name explains their color.) Sunrise shells are rare and hard to find in one piece, but they are the most stunning shell that any beachcomber can find on Kauai.

I know lots of girls agonize over what outfit to wear to school or on a date. Me? I always obsess over what bathing suit to put on for a surf. I have at least a dozen different choices hanging from knobs on my dresser (ah, the perks of being a surfer who is sponsored by a major clothing company, in my case, Rip Curl). My eye caught something black in my closet: black trousers that I bought at a thrift store just a few days before as part of a Halloween costume. My best friend, Alana, got a pair, too, and we bought funky black shoes to match. We would be the "Mexican Mafia," a costume idea we just made up because it sounded silly, and we'd go dressed alike to the Halloween party at church and then off around the neighborhood. Then it hit me: today *is* Halloween.

Halloween in Hawaii is a little complicated. Unlike on the mainland, where people carve their pumpkins a week before the holiday, here it's so warm and humid you only get a day or two to display carved pumpkins before they grow a moldy beard or cave in on themselves in a slimy mess of goo.

While I got ready, the rest of my family was waking up, too. I could hear my dad, Tom, banging around in his bedroom upstairs. A lot of times my father would go surfing with me (he and Mom were the ones who taught me to surf), but today he was going into the hospital for an operation on his knee. The surgery wasn't supposed to be very complicated—he wouldn't even stay in the hospital for the night. Still, someone—my mom, or one of my two older brothers, Noah or Timmy—would have to take him there and drive him home.

I put on a red-white-and-blue bathing suit (to match my red-white-and-blue surfboard) and came from my downstairs room into the living room. My mom was already waiting with her keys, purse, sunglasses, video camera, and a bowl of raisin bran for me to eat on the road. I think she gets as excited as I do about surfing. That's because from the time she was my age, she's been a surf nut too.

"There isn't much showing on the buoys," she informed me. "Maybe we should check Pauaeaka, I heard it was pretty good there yesterday."

Actually, I like Pauaeaka a lot. Pauaeaka is a surf spot located almost at the end of the road on the North Shore of Kauai. It gets its name from the circular shape of the waves, and also because it's really fast and has a hollow wave so sometimes the ride feels just like you're exploding out of a cannon. It's for experts only, because the waves can be very powerful and a bit dangerous.

Surfers judge the quality of a wave by its shape; the more the top or crest throws out to the bottom of the wave, the better. This makes the wave form a little hole that a surfer can pull into, called the "tube." The quality is also judged by the length of the wave; a wave that breaks in a line is much better than a wave that breaks all at once, and Pauaeaka has both a good shape and a long ride.

My dog, Ginger, tried to come with us to Pauaeaka—she always wishes she could come along for the ride—so I scooted her back inside and then tried to find my rubber slippers (people on the mainland call them flip-flops). They were buried in the pile of shoes outside our front door. Taking off your shoes before you go into the house is a firm custom in Hawaii. Nobody has shoes in their closet; they are all out on the front porch. This tradition is probably something left over from the early Hawaiian days or something the Japanese immigrants who moved here a long time ago to work in the cane fields brought with them.

It was still very dark when we jumped into our "Beater." Many people think that surfers drive around in those old wood-paneled station wagons like they see in surfer magazines or in old Beach Boys videos. In truth, most hardcore surfers in

Hawaii drive what everyone calls a "surf beater." It's an older model car with lots of rust, faded paint, and if you're real lucky, free cockroaches! These are the kinds of cars that you don't mind loading with sand, wet towels, bathing suits, melted wax, and surfboards. It just kind of contributes to the car's charisma. Ours is a 1988 Dodge Caravan with a cracked front window (from being knocked hard by a too-long surfboard) that my dad purchased for three hundred dollars. He tried to protect it against rust (not too successfully!) with a thick blue Earl Scheib Paint job.

"What a beast!" my mom declared after seeing Dad's handiwork. We then decided to nickname it the "Blue Crush" after the all-girl surf movie. That, and the fact that we always crush everything into it: family, friends, and gear.

Our car may be junky, but at least the stereo works well. My brothers and I are all into music. I like Switchfoot, 12 Stones, and modern worship music. My mom likes it too. On this morning, we decided to put in a CD by the David Crowder Band. I turned it up when the song "O Praise Him" started playing. "Just don't blast it," Mom reminded me. "We don't want to wake up the whole neighborhood."

We splashed through a lot of puddles left over from the rain as we drove slowly along our North Shore town called Princeville. It was quiet and pitch black as we headed down the windy road that leads from the bluffs to the surf spots in and around Hanalei Bay. We clattered across the old one-car steel bridge that marks the official start of the North Shore. The bridge is too narrow and low for big trucks, so this part of the island has only cars on the road. Sometimes heavy rains close this bridge, stranding everyone who lives past it. Personally, I think kids who live there don't mind at all: they get to miss school!

In the darkness we passed lots and lots of surf spots: the Bay, the Bowl, Pavilions, Pine Trees, Middles, Chicken Wings, Wai Koko. We were headed for the very end of the road called

Pauaeaka. Even though it was dark, with the windows down we could smell the beauty of Hawaii: perfumed plumeria and pikake flowers, the wet earth, grass, and salty air. I took a deep breath and closed my eyes so I could picture it in my mind's eye. Hawaii has this ability to reach out and stir all your senses. It's truly a magical place, and I wouldn't live anywhere else on the planet. I looked over at my mom, who was smiling as well—she felt the same way I did about our home.

We drove past the old Waioli Church and the mission house where some of the first missionaries to Hawaii lived, worked, and died. Finally, we crossed over a very narrow wood bridge that marked the end of our journey.

the calm before the attack

The sun wasn't even up yet. I got out of the car to take a look but it was too dark to see the water. I couldn't hear much either. If the surf is really big, you can actually hear it crashing on the reef from a long way away. "It doesn't seem like much is happening," I told my mom.

Pretty soon the sky east of us began to lighten, and I could see that the surf wasn't anything like it had been the day before. The small waves dumped right onto a sharp coral reef instead of barreling past it. I was itching to get on my board, but the water was just not going to cooperate. If you surf a lot, you get used to this kind of thing. This island has some of the best waves in the world but my friends and I still get skunked sometimes. There is nothing you can do about it; just go home and do something else.

"I guess we should head back," Mom sighed. She was equally disappointed. "Maybe the surf will come up tomorrow." I knew that if I didn't surf I would be home doing social studies, English, or math. Even though I'm working to be a pro surfer and get to be homeschooled in order to help with those goals, my parents pile on the homework.

As we were driving away, I gave it one last

shot: "Let's just check out Tunnels Beach," I suggested. Tunnels is a short walk from Pauaeaka. It's called Tunnels because of all the sand-filled alleys that run through the shallow part of the reef. For tourists it's a popular place to snorkel. Surfers like it because way out on the edge of the reef is a lightning-fast wave that is good both winter and summer.

"Sure, we can go take a look," Mom replied. She did a wild U-turn under the trees and pulled into the last space in the parking lot. While she waited, I walked down the little sand path and watched the waves for a while. Still nothing much. And I didn't really want to paddle out by myself. So I figured that I was doomed to schoolwork and trudged back to the Blue Crush. Suddenly a black pickup truck turned into the parking lot. It was Alana Blanchard, my best friend, her sixteen-year-old brother, Byron, and her dad, Holt. They, like me, were on a mission to find something to surf in.

"Okay," I thought, maybe this wouldn't be a total washout after all. Even though the wave conditions were crummy, everything else was working: it was sunny, the water was warm, and my friends were here to hang with.

"Can I stay, Mom?" I asked. "We think we'll paddle out for some small waves." Why not make the best of it?

"Just make sure Holt brings you home" she called, and with that, I raced down the jungle trail with my friends to Tunnels Beach. I dug my toes into the warm sand and watched the rising sun illuminate the blue sea. Amazingly, the rain hadn't clouded the waters here. Even with all mud-filled rivers pouring into other surf spots, it was as clear as glass.

I glanced over to see Holt putting wax on his board (to keep his feet from slipping). I put the surfboard leash on my left foot, and my Tim Carroll surfboard under my arm. I was happy that I was going surfing; I was happy to be with my friends. I felt the warm water slosh against my ankles, and just before I jumped in, I looked at my watch.

It was 6:40 on a beautiful Halloween morning.

2

roots

A lot of who I am comes from my parents. They're incredible people who've always worked very hard to reach their goals. I know a lot of teenagers think their parents are total aliens from another planet, but I actually think mine are pretty cool. They not only support me in everything I want to do, but they also really inspire me to be a great surfer and even more important, a great human being.

My dad was the ultimate surfer nut. Picture this (when I do, it cracks me up!): it's the dead of winter in Ocean City, New Jersey. Icicles are hanging from the edges of buildings, and the snow is swirling around the sidewalks, rapidly burying the curbs and making huge mounds against the buildings. Everyone is bundled against the cold and scraping the ice off their car windows. Along comes my dad, Tom Hamilton, this skinny seventeen-year-old, trudging through the snowbanks with a surfboard on his head and his beaver tail hat (à la Davy Crockett!) flapping behind him. Dressed in a primitive thick, black diving wetsuit, he would grease his armpits with thick Vaseline to ward off wetsuit rash. And looking like the Creature from the Black Lagoon, he would head out—blizzard and all—to his favorite Ocean City surf spot, Tenth Street.

There he'd meet up with his best buddy, Monk, and the two of them would cross a deserted beach, frosted white, to surf the icy gray Atlantic in conditions so severe that their eyebrows would often freeze solid. Tom and Monk started surfing together as little kids, around age thirteen and fourteen, in the summer of 1962. Within a few years, both boys were dedicated fanatics who took their sport seriously year-round.

"In the winter we would do anything we

could think of to keep warm," my dad has told me. "There were no leashes on surfboards, so if you fell off during the winter months the swim to the beach was brutally cold. We came up with the idea to pour hot water down our wetsuits before going surfing to give us a little edge in the cold. We would be steaming like teakettles all the way to the beach."

I always wondered how my dad knew he was born to be a surfer. When I ask him, he says it was more like destiny took him by the hand and led him to the waves. His parents, George and Mary Hamilton, moved with their four kids around New Jersey a few times before settling in Ocean City. While George set up his dental practice, Mary made sure that my dad and his two brothers and his sister were deeply involved in the sport of swimming.

One day, my grandpa, "Dr. George," brought home a surfboard for my dad. It was a factory-produced pop-out model (as opposed to a normal hand-shaped surfboard) that was on sale at, of all places, a hardware store. One try and Dad was hooked. Soon he and Monk were part of the regular surf scene on the Jersey shore. If Grandpa had only known the daily ritual he created!

moving on

In 1968 my dad graduated from Ocean City High School. As a graduation gift, my grandparents sent him to Manhattan Beach, California, so he could spend the summer surfing. This was the best gift he could ever have imagined. There he prowled up and down the coast tasting firsthand the waves he had only heard about in magazines. But there was a war on. Student deferments were ending, and eighteen-year-old boys everywhere were being drafted and shipped off to the jungles of Vietnam. My dad, hoping that he could find a way to stay around and surf a bit more, joined the reserves but found his unit quickly activated. So, hoping to stick close to the water, he enlisted in the navy.

In 1970 he was sent to Vietnam, and his job was to blast the ship's big guns in support of troop movements. That powerful noise would damage his hearing for life. And though it was not exactly the place that a surfer kid imagined himself winding up, this too proved to be fate.

On his ship, Dad met a young sailor named Robby from Hawaii. Since they both loved surfing, they immediately bonded. Dad was awestruck by the incredible surfing tales Robby would spin. "When this thing is over," Robby kept telling him, "You come to Hawaii!"

During Christmas of 1971, Dad made his first visit to the islands. It was love at first sight. Who could resist the warm tropical trade winds, the transparent, inviting water, the powerful winter waves and the casual, relaxed lifestyle? "One day . . ." he told Robby—making a wish on the waves. Because at that time, since he had completed his service, California was home. He settled in San Diego, enrolled in Mesa Junior College, and, of course, spent all of his free time surfing along the reef-lined Sunset Cliff area.

But it wasn't easy to keep his mind on his studies. His thoughts were someplace far away; he was consumed with getting back to Hawaii. And after two semesters, with my grandparents insisting he had lost his mind, Dad quit school, took the little savings he had from his part-time job, a backpack, and a surfboard, and caught a one-way flight to Hawaii.

He ended up on the island of Kauai. From the airport, Dad hitchhiked to the North Shore, catching a ride in the back of an old red pickup truck filled with buckets of pig slop. The jungles outside Hanalei town had been taken over by a strange breed of hippie surfers. Some, like future world champion Margo Oberg and her husband, Steve, had actually built comfortable and substantial tree houses out of scrap wood and plastic tarp. Others lived a more gritty existence in mildewing tents or rough makeshift shelters. The place was called Taylor's Camp, because the land these squatters lived on was owned by a relative of actress Elizabeth Taylor.

My dad was new to Hawaii, and admittedly pretty clueless. Anxious to get settled and get surfing, he selected a nice ditch to call home. He built a wooden platform for his tent and went surfing every day at Pauaeaka, Tunnels, or at the huge point waves wrapping into Hanalei Bay. But early in rainy season he learned his first lesson: The ditch was really a dormant riverbed, and when he returned from surfing he found that his "home" and all of his belongings had been washed away!

a perfect match...a world away

Around the time my dad was thawing out his frost-bitten toes in New Jersey, on the other end of the continent, in the warm California sun, my mom, Cheri Lynch, and her older sister, Debbie, were slowly dragging a heavy rented surfboard across the sand in Mission Beach, a funky seafront community just north of San Diego. My mom was just twelve, and she could barely wrap her arms around the massive board. She pushed the long, thick hunk of foam and resin toward the horizon, stumbling from time to time in small underwater potholes the current had dug in the sand.

When my mom talks about that moment— her first time surfing—it's as if she's living it all over again. For anyone who truly is a surfer, it's the greatest thrill on earth. I like to hear her talk about it, how she did it, and how she felt: When the water had reached her waist, she swung the nose of the board toward shore and then awkwardly lumbered on board and started to paddle. A rush of rolling white water picked up the surfboard and raced it toward the sand. She rose to her feet, and in a wide beginner stance, rode her first and last wave of the day all the way to the beach. "It was a monumental moment in my life," she often tells me. And I know what she means.

Surfing is an addiction, a pleasure rush indescribable to anyone who has not experienced it. And when it grabs you, it won't let go.

My mom drove her parents crazy with pleas to drive her the twenty minutes down Interstate 8 to the surf rolling in at the foot of Law Street in Pacific Beach. Luckily, my grandparents loved the sand and surf as well. My grandpa, John Lynch, was a football and wrestling coach at San Diego High School. And since his summer schedule was light, it was easy to load up the family (my grandma, Dorothy, Mom, and Aunts Debbie and Karen) into the car and spend the long summer days at the beach.

When not surfing, Mom would snorkel over the kelp-covered reefs of La Jolla searching for legal-size abalone, which they would pop off the rocks with an ab iron. Mom was a daredevil. Some days she and her sisters would spend the afternoon at Marine Street and join others in the lunatic fringe sport of "body whomping" (a crazy kind of body surfing where, if one is not careful, the shallow draining wave will smack its rider into the dry sand bottom with a "whomp!")

Back in her day, girl surfers were a rarity. It was a boys' club, mainly because the early surfboards were heavy and unwieldy. Strong swimming skills were mandatory and leashes were not used. You had to be a real athlete—and she was— to surf with the guys. And frankly, the men didn't mind at all: "I never had to carry my heavy yellow 9'6" surfboard to or from the beach," my mom likes to brag, "There was always a bunch of boys around who were more than willing to help."

When mom graduated she moved to Planet Central for anyone in the hippie, surf, and weirdo scene: Ocean Beach. But she, too, was on her way to Kauai. After pinballing around Southern California, and doing a short-lived detour into the skiing culture of Mammoth Mountain, California, she decided she needed a less hectic lifestyle and a more challenging surf. Kauai, in the early '70s, had not yet been discovered by most tourists but Hollywood had already come knocking. Elvis made a movie there *(Blue Hawaii)* in 1961. And in 1958 Mitzi Gaynor and John Kerr used the North Shore as a backdrop for the film version of the Rodgers & Hammerstein musical *South Pacific*. But for the most part, it was slow-paced, rural, and rich in Hawaiian tradition.

My mom, tired of traveling alone, had talked a casual friend, Chris, into joining her on the adventure. She arrived at the small airport in Lihue, her gear unloaded directly in front of her on slanted steel-covered tables. Weighed down with surfboards and backpacks, the pair made their way to the main highway with the intention of hitchhiking the thirty miles to the North Shore. It took eight hours before a VW van full of surfers finally allowed them to pile in.

Mom had some money saved up so she was able to surf and camp. She immediately found the surfing conditions on Kauai much bigger than anything she was used to in California. She spent her days developing her skill in the large waves and her nights around a campfire with many other surfing expatriates and hippie characters who had migrated to the shores of Kauai.

ladybug and tunas get acquainted

My dad got a job as a banquet waiter at the Kauai Surf Hotel. The hotel was located in the town of Lihue, quite a way from his tent on the North Shore. Since he had no car, he would hitchhike to and from work. But getting a ride home late at night was difficult. There were times when he only got halfway home. Shuffling through some small town at two in the morning, miles from his final location, he would occasionally creep into a local church and sleep on the pews, wrapping himself with the preacher's robe when he got cold.

The North Shore is almost like a small town. Everyone comes to know your neighbors. It didn't take long for my dad to notice the pretty blonde who had been given the nickname Ladybug by her fellow surfers. (He had a nickname as well. He was called Tunas because he used to swim laps in the ocean during his breaks in work so often that everyone said he was like a tuna fish.)

But Mom wasn't interested. She had a boyfriend at the time. She and my dad became friends, but that was it. Until one day, Mom will say, "I didn't have a boyfriend anymore. And things started to happen . . ."

On the following Valentine's Day, which is also my mom's birthday, dad popped the question. "Your mother burst into tears . . . then she married me six months later," Dad explains. And it was a given that any children this couple would have would be quickly introduced to the sport that both their parents loved.

There was, after all, saltwater in the bloodline.

a serious competitor

"**T**wo brothers!"

That's my answer when people ask me why I am *so* competitive. After all, when you're the youngest of three kids *and* the only girl, you kind of have to learn to hold your own. But besides the whole anything-you-can-do-I-can-do-better thing going on between us, my brothers really did inspire me. They're both so different. Noah is twenty-one and a stand-up surfer—just like my mom, my dad, and me. He's pretty skinny, and very quick on the waves. He's also into still photography. He shot most of the great pictures I have of me surfing. What do I admire most about him? When he gets into something he goes all the way. He is very determined and focused.

My brother Timmy is seventeen and he enjoys being the odd guy out—and the class clown. When Noah got into surfing, Timmy decided to be a body boarder. A body board is a hunk of soft foam just over a yard long that is used like a surfboard, except you don't stand up on it. Body boards don't have fins on the bottom; they have hard edges that are used to control turns. Body boarders wear swim fins to help them catch waves with their smaller boards.

Many stand-up surfers don't give body boarders any respect. They call them "spongers" and ignore them in the water or even try to take waves from them. But a good body boarder can really put on an impressive show. They get deeper in the tube than surfers do, take off later, and do crazy aerial stunts. So you can see why Timmy was drawn to it—crazy stunts are his specialty!

Timmy can always crack me up—that's how he is with everyone. He has this natural talent for knowing *exactly* what to do or say, that one thing that will put a smile on your face no matter how grave or serious the situation. He'll do anything—and I mean anything—for a laugh. For example, after my attack, a national TV show was interviewing him, and he was acting all goofy and grooming his hair on-camera. "Who cares if the world thinks I'm nuts?" he told me when I teased him about it. He just wanted to make sure his buddies back home were laughing at Timmy the maniac on TV! But Timmy is more than just funny—he does all the editing to the hours of video my Mom and Dad take of me surfing. He gets really creative and puts cool music to the pictures.

one tough girl

My brothers play very aggressive sports such as roller hockey, soccer, and paintball. When people pick sides, everyone wants my brothers on their team because they are so fast and fierce!

When I saw them playing all these sports, I of course had to play along. I mean why should they have all the fun? And to their credit, they always let me, and never treated me like a little girl. I was one of the boys, and if it meant I got tackled or tumbled or bruised, then that came with the territory. Besides, I could take it! They knew that they could get me to try stuff like in-line skating and skateboarding and I wouldn't back away or cry if I went down.

My brothers pushed me to try things that I might not have done on my own. It was my brothers Timmy and Noah who got me to start surfing Pauaeaka. Honestly, at the time it would have been too scary for me without their encouragement and their absolute faith that I could do it, no sweat!

My brothers cheer me on and are really rooting for me to become a top woman's surfer. My family is like that: when one of us wins a contest or a prize, it's like all of us won, because we all supported each other and helped get that person to the place where they could win.

We were also taught to be good losers. No

matter how good you are, sooner or later you or your team is going to lose. Dad would tell us, "There's no sense in getting upset or being sore. There's always another opportunity to show you can do it." So that's what I try to remind myself if I blow a competition. It's over; move on. Tomorrow's another day.

Even though I've surfed ever since I was five years old, I played other sports, too. I started soccer when I was in the first grade with a team of North Shore girls. For a long time I was put in a defensive position, a sweeper. At first I was disappointed. I desperately wanted to be the one to score the goal during the game. Then I realized that the coach put me where I was for a reason. I had quick reflexes and was a good blocker. One thing I learned about team sports: no one job is more more important than the others. You all have to work together. I played soccer for six years before getting the chance to score that goal. That's a long time, I know, but it just made scoring even sweeter.

my first big win

My parents started signing me up for surf competitions while I was still in grade school. Most of these contests were "push and ride" types of competitions where a parent will push the kid into a wave instead of the kid having to try and catch the wave themselves.

By the time I was seven years old I was able to surf and catch waves without my parents' help. I still needed to be coached, but I was getting better and better every day. With my parents' support, I decided to enter the Rell Sun contest on the island of Oahu. This was big, especially for an eight-year-old kid.

Traveling around the State of Hawaii isn't all that easy or cheap. We had to come up with money for the entry fee, airline tickets, car rental, food, and hotel costs. And unlike with golf or some other sport, if you win, there is little or no money, especially in the kid and girl divisions.

The contest was being held at Makaha Beach. There were lots of great surfers there, and as I looked around, I felt superexcited to be with everyone. The surfing community, especially in the kids' division, is like one big happy family.

The waves were big and I could feel the adrenaline rush. A lot of young kids get intimidated when the surf starts getting huge. Me? I live for it—the bigger the better! Makaha was not a place I had ever surfed before, and that gave the advantage to local kids, who knew the spot better. But I didn't let that scare me either.

I entered in two divisions, the girls ages seven to nine short board, and the seven to nine long board. The oldest kid in the contest was twelve, because the Rell Sun contest is designed to be for kids under thirteen, or "groms," as they are called in the surfing world.

One of the girls surfing that day, Carrisa Moore, was really good and I admired her toughness. She would have won the contest but she had an accident that actually put a deep cut on her throat with the fin of her surfboard. We were at the contest with a bunch of other Christian families, so we all got together and prayed for her.

things get rolling

Then it was time for my heat. My mom told me where to take off. I surfed pretty well that day and ended up winning all my heats and the division championships. My prize, other than trophies, was two brand new surfboards. Guys who were surf legends presented me with them while my friends and family gathered around and cheered. I was pretty stoked. And I remember thinking, "Is this really happening to *me?*"

Winning that contest kind of got things rolling for me. I entered more and more contests and did pretty well in most of them. I entered the Haleiwa Menehune Contest, which is held on the famous North Shore of Oahu. (Menehunes are a legendary race of little bitty people in Hawaiian folklore.) I found that I was competing against the same kids as before, which was great, because we all got to know each other, and I made some great new friends. These contests, while competitive in the water, are actually fun, happy events where winning is secondary to enjoying the surf, the beach, and all the companionship.

And no one really gets cocky like in other competitive sports. There's no, "I'm the best and you can't touch me." Because we all know so many things can happen while you are in the water: nature can play games with you, or your timing can simply be off. So anyone can take home a trophy—and if you lose, there's always tomorrow.

A lot of times I have to surf in the same heat as my friend Alana. We both try hard to beat each other. There are never any hard feelings from the one that loses, and we are happy for the other if she wins. It's just a sport, nothing to get all stressed out about. Today, I have the same attitude, although as I get older, the contest scene gets a bit more intense. The stakes are higher: bigger money, more sponsorship and endorsement deals.

As I started winning more contests, it seemed possible that I might be able to become a professional surfer as a couple of other girls from my island have done. At least my parents and my brothers thought so. I didn't let my head go there right away. Instead, I just wanted to enjoy the moments while I was living them and not worry too much about the future.

My brother Noah became my promoter. He created a great résumé for me and mailed it off to various surf companies. He set up Web sites and computer programs; he takes photos and even helps me with surfboard design so that I will get a board made specifically for the kind of surfing I do. He contacted surf gear and clothing companies and he sent promotional packs to anyone in the surfing industry he could think of. Since he loves surf photography and went to college to study business, he's a natural salesman. He was the one who helped me get my sponsor: Rip Curl.

People ask me all the time my secret to winning a competition. Beats me. All I can tell you is that it's a combination of perfecting your skill and keeping a positive outlook. I don't get nervous or stressed out before a contest. In fact, other than going out and surfing the spot before the contest, I don't even think about it much. I study the waves briefly before a contest to help me plot my strategy. Based on what I observe, I pick out a marker on the beach to line up with, and figure out the best place to take off.

Sometimes I make a bad move, and when I do, and I lose a heat as a result, I have to admit I get bummed out and down on myself. "Bethany, you have to get over it," my dad will tell me. So I take his advice and try to shake it off so that I can focus on what's ahead. He has also taught me the importance of learning from my mistakes. I make sure to break any bad habits before they begin.

Because I'm still an amateur, I don't get money for winning a contest but I do have the opportunity to make money from my sponsors if I place high. But dollar signs aren't what it's all about for me. Once in a while, someone forgets that a surf contest is really about having fun, and that really spoils it for everyone. I hate to feel that negative energy. At one contest, a dad was screaming at his daughter because she wasn't surfing well. I felt really bad for her. What does that accomplish anyway? Wouldn't a little encouragement have worked better?

My family is great on that front: they're my number one fans. Win or lose, they think I'm awesome, and I know I have their love and support no matter how I place in a contest. Both my folks just dabbled in competition, and neither of my brothers cares to enter contests. So I guess that makes me the star competitor of the family—not that it gets me out of doing my chores at home!

My favorite surf spots are:

Pine Trees—Hanalei, Kauai, Hawaii

Trussels—San Clemente, California

Bells Tourquay—Australia

Popoya-Santana—Nicaragua

And my FAVORITE . . .

Hanalei Pier—In Kauai, where I learned!

make way for the women

More and more girls have started surfing, which means that they are finally being taken seriously as athletes and can actually make a living at this sport, something that was nearly impossible a decade ago. Today, there are even magazines aimed specifically toward women surfers.

Women on the pro surf tour are a very tight-knit bunch, and they're all very dedicated. The girls on the amateur circuit (which is what I surf) are on pretty good terms as well, although there are a lot more of us nowadays, so I can't say I'm tight with everyone just yet. But I love to meet new people and get to know them.

I don't know what other girls do before they go out in a heat, but for me the routine is pretty simple: I pray. I pray for safety for everyone and I pray for wisdom in my wave selection and the ability to be at the right place at the right time.

People often ask me if I had ever been hurt surfing before my accident. Actually surfing is a pretty safe sport: if you fall, you hit water, which is much better than, say, being a skateboarder and smacking down on the hard pavement. Once or twice I got held down for a long time in big surf. This is not really the same as getting hurt, but for a few minutes you become a little panicky and the thought "I might drown" enters your mind. Then the wave lets you up again and you can breathe and you forgot you were scared.

Most surfers get injured from their own surfboard or someone else's board. Once I was playing in the shorebreak and got slammed by my board. It hurt so bad that I stayed out of the water for several days. You know it would take a lot to keep me from surfing—I was one big bruise. Other times, a big wave will bounce you off the bottom, and if the bottom happens to be coral . . . well, let's just say that you're not a pretty sight with all those cuts and slices.

Bumps, bruises, reef rash . . . hey, it comes with the territory. I'll take it all and then some. . . . as long as I can surf.

4

a mostly normal life

I have a mostly normal life.

Mostly normal because I have a lot of the same interests as most fourteen-year-olds: music, movies, and driving my older brothers crazy. But in some ways my life is pretty different. Take for instance living three thousand miles from the rest of the United States.

Having a home on a tiny island in the middle of the Pacific Ocean isn't for everybody. There are no big shopping malls, only a couple of movie theaters, no ice-skating rinks, no miniature golf or go-cart places. We have only one road to get around on, and if there is a traffic accident half the island can be blocked from getting anywhere for a long, long time.

It's such a small place that you get to know lots of people and can have friends all over the island. We always joke that if a kid gets in trouble in school, the parents know about it before the kid gets off the school bus. But the smallness also has its advantages: if your car breaks down on the side of the road, chances are good that someone you know will come by real soon and help out.

People who have lived their whole life in a big city don't always understand what my life here is like—or why I wouldn't want to, say, move to L.A. or New York or some other fast-paced city where there's lots of action and excitement. Here's what I think: you make your own adventure in life. And I truly believe that if you open your eyes to your surroundings, there's lots of neat stuff to be found practically anywhere on earth. For me, the grass is never greener outside of Hawaii. If you ask me my favorite things about my home, I can think of dozens. But my top three are pretty easy:

1. **It's never cold.** I wear shorts and a T-shirt almost all year long. It's even warm at Christmastime. In fact, our family Christmas tradition is to get up early and go surfing and then come back and open gifts. We like to do this because there are almost always good waves that time of year, and the best surf spots are uncrowded because everyone else is home looking under the tree!

2. **There's always something to do.** Especially if you love the sand and surf like I do. When there are no waves or when I am done surfing I like to pick shells on the beach, snorkel over the reef, swim around with the sea turtles, or go swimming at a natural lava rock swimming pool called Queen's Bath, which is filled every high tide with saltwater. Sometimes my friends and I hike to the waterfall at Hanakapi'ia.

3. **Bananas and papayas.** They grow all over the place here, even in my backyard. And honestly, I could eat them for breakfast, lunch, and dinner seven days a week. There is nothing

like a papaya right off the tree, ripe and ready to eat. I'm a pretty good smoothie chef: my papaya smoothies are legendary and I do tend to add papaya to almost every dish (it just makes it taste better). Which isn't to say I'm a health food freak. Far from it: I have a soft spot for vanilla ice cream with sliced bananas sprinkled with cinnamon, root beer floats, and chocolate!

That said, the rest of my life here probably won't sound that out of the ordinary to you. I like to watch old TV programs. One of my favorite shows is *Leave It to Beaver*. I don't know why, but I really like that program. The Beaver is this sweet, innocent kid who's always getting into trouble. He just makes me laugh. I also love to watch *Animal Planet*, *Mr. Ed*, *The Simpsons*, *Malcolm in the Middle*, and *SpongeBob Squarepants*.

Because everybody in the family loves to surf, sometimes we all just sit around watching surf movies. When I say surf movies I am not talking about dumb Hollywood attempts to show surfing, but hard core surf movies that have no plot, just lots and lots of surfing by the world's hottest surfers. And I love to watch the movie *Finding Nemo!*

There is a whole gang of us who do things together: Kayla, Noelane, Michelle, Camille and Jackie, Kaylee, Kyae, Summer, and of course, Alana. At Alana's house we sometimes hose down her trampoline and squirt liquid soap all over it. Then we tie plastic bags on our feet and jump—or try to jump. Usually we end up sliding all over the place laughing our heads off.

When a bunch of us get together we often play an old street game called kick the can. One time, the can got kicked into a little green area, so we chased it in and started stomping around, until we were in somebody's garden. I don't think they appreciated us wrecking their plants, but we were having such a fun time, I swear we didn't notice!

Once in a while we will play ding-dong ditch. This is a game where you ring somebody's doorbell and then run away as fast as you can so they can't catch you. One time we played this on Andy Irons, who had just won the world title in surfing and lives a few doors away from Alana. He finally caught us but he wasn't mad. Probably 'cause he used to do the same thing a few years ago when he was a teenager.

I consider myself quite the practical joker. We do all kinds of crazy pranks at our winter camp, like raiding the boys with shaving cream. Once in a while, I get in trouble for getting a little out of hand and have to go and apologize. But the guys that run the camp understand because they like to play jokes themselves.

When it rains a lot (and sometimes it rains for a couple of weeks straight) we take body boards and find big, steep, wet, grassy hills to slide down. This is what I like to call tobogganing, Hawaiian style!

Of course I do stuff with my church, the North Shore Community Church. Doing things with my Christian friends is an important part of my life, because it really is encouraging to have others who, like me, want to be close to God.

My parents and brothers are involved in church-related activities as well, but I would go even if they didn't. Every week we have a thing called Rad Nite where we do fun things such as games and relays or barbecues. At the end, our leaders, Sarah Hill and Troy and Maila Gall, lead us in a short Bible study, usually about what Jesus said or did.

We also have camps and retreats that are pretty crazy and interesting too. We combine our church with the youth group from a south side church called Kauai Christian Fellowship. That makes well over a hundred of us middle schoolers! The camps have different themes each year. This year, the staff dressed like pirates and built a ship-wreck on the grounds of the camp. We even put a plank over the swimming pool. The catch: we filled the pool with water and seventy-five pounds of dog food. So if you lost a contest, you had to walk the plank and were in for a disgusting swim! We also play gross games such as turkey football (ever try tossing around an uncooked butterball?). The field is a huge sheet of plastic coated with dishwashing liquid so you slip and slide all the way. But it's not all games. We also have great rock-and-roll worship and great speakers as well as cabin quiet times and devotionals.

Every so often I get to go with my family to the mainland for a vacation. When we do, I really like to go to amusement parks like Six Flags. I discovered I have an iron stomach. I can go on all the rides that spin you in a circle real fast without getting sick. My favorite is the Spin Out: the bottom drops out from underneath you and you're stuck to the wall. My dad will go on most of the roller coaster rides such as the Cyclone or Colossus, but even *he* can't handle the Spin Out.

I homeschool. It makes it easier to be a career surfer and to travel. My mom is my teacher and I get a lot of my assignments online. Typically my workload is just like that of a public high school student with the exception that I can do it on my hours. A lot of my friends are homeschooled as well (such as Alana), so we end up having the same schedule of surfing, traveling, and then homework.

If I were in a regular school I bet my favorite subject would be art (after P.E. of course). I really like to create things. I like to make crafts and use my shells in the design. I've made some cool switch-plate covers out of shells, paint, and other natural material. I really enjoy doing this kind of thing but my surfing and schoolwork have kept me so busy that I have had little time to pursue this hobby.

Sometimes people ask me about boys. Boys are fine, but to be honest, I am *so* busy right now that I don't have any time to think about them.

Music is something that I enjoy a lot too. I have stacks of CDs that I get from my brothers. I really like Switchfoot. Those guys are surfers, Christians, and play the kind of songs that I like, songs that are fun, fast, and kind of punk-sounding, but with lyrics that bring God into the picture. There are a lot of bands from Kauai that are good too. Chandelle and Pennylane are two that I really like. I like modern praise and worship music too. Some people think that music in a church is just dull, organ-led hymns. Forget it! Sure, all the songs are about how great God is and praise him. But the music in our church is real modern: electric guitars, drums, and bass. Most of the songs have a great beat that makes you want to clap and stomp your feet.

Sometimes I feel I have so much going on in one day, I don't know how I pack it all in. I guess it's kind of like what a teenage actor must feel like: you have to get up and go to work, yet still make time to be a kid. When I'm not surfing, I'm training. And when I'm not training, I'm doing homework. Whatever time I have left over (and it's not a lot!), I spend it with friends and family.

People don't often get the whole homeschooling thing. "Bethany," they say, "that's a little weird, isn't it? I mean, don't you miss campus life?" Well, most of my friends are homeschooled; the people I hang with are either surf buddies or kids from my church. So no, it feels totally normal to me. But that doesn't mean that as I get older—I'm starting high school this year—I might miss the opportunities to go to the prom or homecoming or stuff like that. But seriously, there is no way I could go to a regular school and participate in professional surfing. There's only so much of me to go around and only 24 hours in a day! And let me tell you, homeschooling is no way easier than your traditional classroom. I have tests, and a mom who's pretty tough when it comes to making sure I hit those books and pull straight A's.

I never had a lot of free time because of my surfing, and now, after the accident, my schedule is ten times as nuts. For example, this week I flew to California to receive an award, then I headed off to Portugal to be in a Volvo ad.

Fortunately there are waves in both places.

Which now brings us to stuff I don't like. I hate spiders and snakes. We don't have any snakes in Hawaii but whenever I go to the mainland and stay in someplace that has lots of those creepy things, I get so freaked out about them that I can hardly sleep at night! We have humongous centipedes in Hawaii that slither around like snakes and can give you a nasty bite, but just thinking of a *real* snake makes me shudder. Funny, huh? I guess everyone has something that freaks them out.

I hate school lunches . . . yuck! Obviously now that I am homeschooled I don't have to eat them anymore, but for many years I had to choke down burnt chicken sticks, supersugary canned fruit, and potatoes that tasted like plastic. Just the thought of them . . . well, it's worse than snakes!

This all probably sounds pretty ordinary. Most everybody has things they like or dislike, most everybody has a bunch of friends that they hang out with and favorite foods, music, and movies.

And in most ways I am just your typical teenage girl. And in some ways, because of my accident, I'm not. For example, I can't put on certain clothes without getting some help with buttoning. Tying shoes is tough with one hand. Peeling an orange without holding it between my feet is next to impossible.

I don't think much about it or worry about how I look with one arm. People around here know me and don't think much about it either—which saves me having to explain. I could try to hide the fact by wearing my prosthetic arm, but then I would have to wear more clothes because you have to strap it on. Besides, it just kind of hangs there doing nothing, so I don't have much use for it. Maybe I look a little different without it, but that's okay. I'm cool being me.

attack

I didn't even scream.

People say to me, "Weren't you terrified?" "Didn't you think you would be eaten alive?" I guess that would be the normal reaction, but it wasn't mine. Maybe I was in shock or denial; maybe I was on autopilot. I'm not really sure, but when I look back on it now, I'm glad of one thing: I'm glad I never saw the shark closing in on me. I'm glad I never had more than a split second to wrap my brain around the fact that I was being attacked. If I had, I'm not sure I would have been so calm. I'm not sure I'd be able to live with the nightmares or ever go back in the water again . . .

We had only been surfing a half hour and the

waves were nothing spectacular. We were waiting for the next decent one to roll in, and Alana was floating no more than fifteen feet from me; her brother, Byron, and dad, Holt, not much farther away. I was bringing up the rear, and all of us were looking out to sea.

I had a shiny, light blue Rip Curl watch on my left hand that I was dangling in the water. I sometimes wonder if the reflection of that watch in the clear water is what attracted the shark. That's when I was suddenly aware of a large gray object closing in on my left side. He was slow and silent; he really crept up on me. If I had had my head turned I would have seen everything: the rolled-back eyes, the triangle-shaped teeth, the sandpaper-like skin, the pointy snout, the pulled-back gums. Luckily, all I saw was a blur.

It's funny—you would think having your arm bitten off would really hurt. But there was no pain at the time. I felt pressure and kind of a jiggle-jiggle tug, which I know now was the teeth. They have serrated edges like a steak knife and they sawed through the board and my bones as if they were tissue paper.

It was over in a few seconds. I remember seeing the water around me turn bright red with my blood. Then I saw that my arm had been bitten off almost to the shoulder. There was just a three- or four-inch stub where my limb had once been.

My reaction, Alana has told me, was amazingly matter-of-fact and in control. I just said in a kind of loud yet not panicked voice, "I just got attacked by a shark," and started to paddle away with one arm. I knew the shore was a very long quarter of a mile, but one thought kept repeating over and over in my head: "Get to the beach. Get to the beach."

I also wasn't thinking that the shark was going to come back and attack me again. I wasn't trying to swim away from it, and I don't even know if it was still circling the area at the time. Now I realize I could have easily been bitten again and again. Once a shark gets a taste of you, it's been known to come back for more. But this didn't occur to me. "Beach," my mind screamed while my voice was silent. "Get to the beach . . ."

Byron and Holt got to me in a flash. I said out loud, to no one in particular, "I can't believe that this happened." Holt's face was white and his eyes were wide. "Oh, my God!" he said, but he didn't freak out. Instead, he took control of the situation: He pushed me by the tail of my board, and I caught a small wave that washed me over the reef as I lay on my board. It's a small miracle that it was high tide. If it had been low tide, we would have had to go all the way around the reef to get to shore—a trip of a quarter of a mile that usually takes ten minutes to paddle over reef that's twenty to thirty feet in depth. Byron rode the same wave as I did, lying on his belly, pointing straight in to the beach. Whatever emotions Holt, Byron, and Alana were feeling they kept inside; nobody panicked or lost their head.

My arm was bleeding badly, but not spewing blood like it should with a major artery open. I know now that wounds like mine often cause the arteries to roll back, tighten. I wasn't freaking out, but I was praying like crazy, "Please, God, help me. God, let me get to the beach," over and over again. I was afraid, but not of anything specific. Just kind of a general "I've been hurt bad and I don't know what's going to happen to me" kind of fear. Holt took off his gray long sleeve rash guard. The reef was shallow at that point, only a couple of feet deep, so he stood up and tied the rash guard around the stub of my arm really tight to act as a tourniquet.

"Hold on to my shorts and I'll paddle you in," he instructed me. So I grabbed on to the bottom of his swim trunks and held on tight as he paddled both of us toward shore. Byron was already ahead of us, stroking like crazy to the beach to call 911. Holt told me to keep talking to him. He kept having me answer questions like "Bethany, are you still with me? How ya doing?" I think he wanted to make sure that I didn't pass out in the middle of the ocean. So I was talking, although I don't know about what. I think I was just answering his questions and praying out loud and watching that shoreline get closer and closer.

It was during this, the longest part of getting to the beach—those fifteen minutes or so—that the fear began to wash over me. A thought flashed into my mind: "You could die." But I pushed any negative vibes away quickly with a prayer. "I'm in God's hands," I remember thinking, and I forced myself back into the here and now and concentrated on holding on.

I remember seeing Alana. She was paddling next to me like always, looking mostly at the shore but sometimes glancing over to check me out. There was fear in her eyes, but she tried to hide it. As we got closer to the beach, I heard someone say, "Quick! Go get the lifeguard." I knew that it was too early for them to be on duty, so I called out a couple of times, "They aren't on duty!" But I don't know if anybody was listening to me.

land at last

As we got close, Holt got off his board and pushed me the last few feet to the beach. People were gathering all around me, and Holt lifted me off the surfboard and laid me on the sand. At that point, everything went black, and I'm not sure how long I was out of it. I kept coming in and out of consciousness, struggling to make heads or tails of what was going on.

Holt got a leash from Jeff Waba, another surfer who was surfing farther out at Tunnels and had come racing in when he heard what had happened to me. They removed the rash guard and tied the surf leash—which is a lot like surgical tubing—like a tourniquet.

What happened after that is confusing, and it all tends to run together, a mix of sights, sounds, and feelings. Kind of like trying to remember a dream you had: while you're dreaming, it all makes sense. But when you try to recall it, all you get are bits and pieces that don't quite add up.

I remember being cold. I heard this happens when you lose lots of blood. People brought beach towels and wrapped me up in them. Everyone was concerned but they all seemed to be assuring me in some way and trying to help me remain calm and comfortable.

I remember starting to feel pain in my stump and thinking, "This hurts a lot." And I know I said, "I want my mom!" a few times. Funny how when you're scared, no matter how grown up you think you are, you do want your mommy to comfort you.

I remember being very thirsty and asking Alana for water. So she ran up to a visitor, Fred Murray, who was jogging along the beach while the rest of his group, here on Kauai for a family reunion, relaxed at a beachfront rental home. "Come with me!" he yelled, and they both raced back to get one of his family members, a man named Paul Wheeler, who was the captain and a paramedic at a Haywood, California, fire station. "It's my friend, she needs water," said Alana. She explained, as best she could because she was so in shock, what had happened.

Paul didn't hesitate. He bolted out the door to be by my side. "Don't worry," he said, "I can help. I'm a paramedic. Everyone please stand back . . ." I remember his face and the compassion in his voice. I think everyone was relieved that there was a professional on the scene; I know it comforted me to know it. Paul examined the wound and pulled on the tourniquet. At that point, Alana came with water, but Paul advised against it. "I know you're thirsty," he told me, "But you're going to need surgery, and you want an empty stomach."

A neighbor brought a small first-aid kid in a Tupperware container, and Paul slipped on gloves so he could wrap my wound in gauze and feel around some more. I remember wincing as he poked around, but I knew he had to do it. Paul felt my pulse. He shook his head. "She's lost a lot of blood," he said quietly.

I remember a dog getting through the crowd and trying to lick me: he must have been worried about me too.

I remember thinking, "Why is the ambulance taking so long to get here? Please, please hurry!" Byron had broken into the back of his dad's pickup to fish out his cell phone and given all the info to the emergency operator, but no one had arrived yet on the scene. It felt like an eternity, and I could see Byron pacing.

Holt decided we couldn't wait any longer. He and some other surfers lifted me onto Holt's board and carried me to the parking lot, where they put me in the back of his truck. Again, I kept passing out, only catching glimpses of what was going on and bits of frantic conversation.

I remember the sirens of the emergency vehicles, high-pitched and shrill. I remember being stuck with needles and being slid on a stretcher into the back of the ambulance.

I remember most clearly what the Kauai

paramedic said to me: He spoke softly and held my hand as we were pulling out of the Tunnels parking lot. He whispered in my ear, "God will never leave you or forsake you."

He was right.

dark hours

I'm always so anxious to arrive at a surf site that the road to get there—all the tiny bridges and the neck-whipping curves carved along the cliff face—drives me crazy. I wish my mom could go faster, and I often egg her on to speed it up, but I know it's a tough road to navigate, and I have to be patient.

Still, when you're lying in the back of that ambulance, and the driver is carefully taking each corner and bump at a snail's pace, it's impossible to be patient. I knew the trip would take forty-five minutes but it felt like an eternity. It would be a while before we reached the bluffs of Princeville and the road straightened out enough for the driver to step hard on the gas pedal.

I can only imagine what my mom was going through at home at that very moment. Jeff Waba at Tunnels made the call: "Mrs. Hamilton, there's been an accident . . ." He tried to speak calmly and clearly. "You need to go to the hospital. Your daughter has been attacked by a shark." My mom thought that Jeff and I were playing with her head—another one of my practical jokes—and that he would put me on the phone so I could ask for a ride home. "Come on, what's really going on?" she said, skeptically.

Jeff didn't know how to respond: "No, *really*, she's been attacked by a shark!" he said.

This time my mom knew he wasn't joking—she could hear the tension in his voice. She hung up the phone and broke down in tears.

I knew she'd be imagining the worst—that I was dying or in horrible pain—but I also knew she'd be trying to keep her head. She had to. She had to be strong for her family, strong for me. Noah told me she was almost in a trance: she knew what she had to do, namely get to the hospital to be with me, and the only way to do it was to block out all the fear and grief. "I was numb when they told me," she would later confess. "It was like I went into autopilot."

She broke the news to my brother Noah, who was still sleeping downstairs. "Noah, we've got to go to the hospital. Bethany's been attacked by a shark." He asked for details but my mom didn't have any to give. "I'm going to the hospital!" Noah said bolting out of bed. He somehow managed to pull on a T-shirt and pants and at the same time call a family friend, youth counselor Sarah Hill.

Sarah was just pulling into the parking lot at Hanalei Elementary School, where she worked, when her phone rang: "Sarah, Bethany's been attacked by a shark!" Noah sounded breathless and terrified; Sarah tried to remain calm for him, but she couldn't believe her ears. She and I had often surfed together and even though we are years apart, we are really good friends.

For the sake of convenience, they agreed to

meet at the nearby Hanalei police station and travel together to the hospital. Noah needed her.

Jumping into the car with Sarah, Noah then dialed Mike Dennis, a friend who lived near Tunnels, hoping he could fill in the blanks: What condition was I in? Had he seen the ambulance? Mike had heard the sirens but didn't know what had happened. He promised to try to find out and then call back.

Sarah and Noah raced toward the hospital with my mom following close behind in the Beater. I know Noah was a wreck but trying very hard not to let his nerves get to him. Sarah was there for him to lean on. She told him that she had prayed for God to give her a message for our family, and a small verse from the Old Testament zipped into her mind:

"For I know the plans I have for you," declares the Lord, "plans to prosper you and not to harm you, plans to give you hope and a future."

—JEREMIAH 29:11

"You've gotta tell my mom that verse!" Noah said over and over. Maybe God did have something bigger planned for me. What we all needed to do was trust . . . and believe.

the bad news

"She's lost her arm," Mike told Noah a few minutes later. "Oh, my God," cried Noah. "Oh, no! I can't believe it, I can't believe it!" He knew he couldn't tell my mom, not yet. It would be too overwhelming for her to handle without being able to see me with her own two eyes. Instead, he and Sarah started calling all of our Christian friends around the islands to start a chain of prayer.

As my mom reached the ornate fountain that marks the entryway into our Princeville community, they heard the wail of sirens approaching. By the time they got to the stop sign, the ambulance had flown by. Gunning the gas, they fell in behind us, but I had no idea. And I had forgotten my dad was already at the hospital that morning preparing for his own surgery. Knowing my parents were so close to me would have made me feel a little better.

At the hospital, my dad was on the operating table. Rather than be put under, he had opted for an anesthetic that would only numb him from the waist down. His orthopedic surgeon, Dr. David Rovinsky, was preparing to start the operation when an emergency room nurse burst into the room. "Just a heads-up, Dr. Rovinsky," she announced. "There's a thirteen-year-old girl coming, a shark attack victim. We are going to need this room right away."

The doctor, remembering that it was Halloween, thought that the nurse was playing some morbid practical joke. But my dad heard her and knew this was no joke. He also knew in his heart that the thirteen-year-old girl had to be either me or Alana.

"Tom, stay here," the doctor tried to calm him. "I'll go and try to find out what's happening." My poor dad lay there alone on the table, unable to move, praying, worrying, and wondering. He had no cell phone to call my mom; no way of contacting anyone. Within five minutes Dr. Rovinsky returned. His face was pale and there were tears in his eyes. "Tom, it's Bethany," he said softly. "She's in stable condition. That's all I know, I don't have any other information. Tom, I'm going to have to roll you out. Bethany's coming in here."

My dad later told me that that hour in the recovery room was torture: his mind was wild with scenarios of what might be happening to me in that operating room, the room he was supposed to be in. "I tried to will the feeling back into my legs so I could run in there and see you," he admitted. "I had no idea how bad you were—I prayed all you needed were just a few stitches and you'd be good as new." But like his heart had told him I was the one who had been attacked, it also told him it was much worse than a few stitches.

Timmy got the news in first period at Kapaa High School. The cell phone in his backpack chimed. It was Mom: "Timmy, Bethany's going to the hospital." He actually thought Mom was talking about Dad, whom he had just dropped off twenty minutes before. "Um, okay," he replied. He thought maybe his mom was confused and went back to reading his surfing magazine in the library.

The next phone call was from Noah, who was brief but a lot clearer in his description of what had happened: "Timmy, Bethany's been attacked by a shark! Get over to the hospital right now!" Timmy ran to his car while dialing friends to get them to pray for me.

Shortly before reaching the hospital, Holt called Mom on her cell for the first time. She knew nothing except that I was hurt. Holt had to tell her the shocking news: "Cheri, she's lost an arm." Mom said she dropped the phone, pulled the Blue Crush over to the edge of the road, stared at her two hands on the steering wheel, and broke down weeping.

My mom was crushed. All the work and effort we were putting into my future as a pro seemed to her at that moment to be washed away. Still, in spite of her tears and heartbreak, she had the presence of mind to turn on a worship CD and sing along with it. Through her tears and pain, she praised God and told him that in spite of everything, He was in control. I was in His hands.

chaos and concern

I was in surgery, so I was completely removed from the circus that was going on in the waiting room: family and friends desperately trying to figure out what condition I was in; crying, pacing, praying. I knew my mom would be grabbing any nurse or doctor she could get her hands on, begging for an update, and I knew that Noah's stomach would be totally topsy-turvy (he later admitted that he threw up as soon as they got out of the car). Thankfully, Timmy found Dad in recovery and filled him in on the little he knew: at least he reassured him I was still alive. Eventually Dad was able to move his legs, and an attendant came in and, seeing him sitting upright in a chair, asked if he wanted to see me.

He didn't wait for any help: he dragged himself out of that room, looking for me.

surgery

The medics called it a "traumatic amputation." I was lucky, because on duty that morning at Wilcox was Dr. Ken Pierce, the same emergency room doctor who had handled the foot amputation by a tiger shark of body boarder Mike Coots a few years earlier.

Dr. Pierce received a call by radio that there was a shark attack victim in the area of Tunnels Beach. Knowing the distance involved, he knew that he would have plenty of time to prepare. A short while later the paramedics radioed in, telling the ER the rest of the story: "It's a thirteen-year-old female and the arm is gone . . ."

Dr. Pierce—an avid surfer himself who knew me well through our sport and also our church—

later told me he had a premonition that it was me. It made sense: there were few young girls who would be surfing Tunnels on a school day. But more than that, his gut was telling him it *was* me, and this would be a very tough operation personally and professionally.

When the paramedics wheeled me into the emergency room, my dad's doctor, Dr. Rovinsky, said I was "cool as a cucumber." All I know is that there was an incredible relief in knowing I was in a hospital where people could help me. I had made it this far . . . I was going to survive this. I was awake but a little sleepy when I arrived. They whisked me into a room before I could see anyone.

The other bizarre thing: I really wasn't in pain. Dr. Pierce has this theory about that. He says that minor injuries produce pain as a warning for the body to "watch out" or nurse the injured part. But in the case of a severe injury, the body's nerve endings virtually shut down, knowing instinctually that the body does not need to be warned of danger because danger has already arrived, and directing all the resources of the body to be focused on trying to stay alive.

So they hooked me up to lots of machines—I'm not sure what they all were for, but I know they were giving me fluids and taking lots of X-rays and blood levels. Later I would learn that I had lost nearly half of my blood volume.

It was Dr. Rovinsky who would be doing the first surgery (orthopedic surgeons do all the amputations at Wilcox), and he explained to both me and Mom how he would do it. "You've lost your arm, Bethany," he said gently, "now the focus is on saving your life." He stressed that he was going to try to leave me as much of my arm as possible and that I would be going to the operating room and would be knocked out for the surgery.

According to Dr. Rovinsky, shark bites, and particularly tiger shark bites, tend to have a high risk of infection because these scavengers' mouths are pretty filthy. So he had to thoroughly clean the wound. Then he'd find the nerves and cut them, causing them to retract and reduce the potential for the phenomenon called phantom pain—the sharp feeling of ache in a portion of a limb that no longer exists in reality but still sends signals to the brain. The wound would then be left open but packed with gauze for several days to ensure that there was no infection. Dr. Pierce would do the second surgery to close the wound, using a flap of my skin.

the work begins

"Do you want anything?" the nurse asked me.

"Just to go to sleep," I said.

I was tired from the loss of blood. I was tired from the trauma and from being poked and prodded by doctors and medics. I remember a kind nurse saying, "Okay, Bethany. Close your eyes and sleep." I did, and gently drifted off as if I had been in my own bed. No last prayers, not even any big worries, just peace and relief.

I had a good feeling about Dr. Rovinsky. When he spoke, he was both kind and confident, and he was also a surfer and a friend of my father. He said things would be okay. He assured my mom that the odds were in my favor: I was young, in great physical shape, the cut had been direct rather than a ragged tear, and my calmness had kept my heartbeat slow enough to keep the severed artery from quickly draining my blood supply. Holt's great tourniquet and everyone's quick reaction had also been a big plus. "Look," he told her, "a lot of things had to have gone right for her to make it to this point. She's got everything going for her."

He also was optimistic that I would be able to compensate well with one arm in the future. In fact, he figured that even the idea of a prosthetic arm might have a fifty-fifty chance of being practical. "A lot of kids get used to making do without the missing limb," he told my mother. "And Bethany is a fighter."

the road back

I have a few very vivid memories of things that took place after I first arrived at the hospital and the few days I spent there recovering. For one, I was terribly thirsty. I had nothing to drink all morning and only a bowl of raisin bran for breakfast. I was real thirsty on the beach and nobody would give me any water because I was headed for the hospital. As soon as I got there, I was rushed to X-ray rooms and the whole time I was dying for a drink of water.

When I finally saw Timmy before my surgery, I started saying over and over again, "Get me water, get me water." I guess I must have sounded delirious, because Timmy looked at me like I was crazy. But he finally ran and got me some. I drank it down like a person who has been in the desert for days! They gave me cup after cup. But I don't think they asked the doctor if they should.

As soon as I came out from under the anesthesia I barfed; water and raisin bran, yuck! Then I saw my dad. I was supergroggy, but I said, "Hi, Dad, glad you're here." My dad says that I had an "everything is going to be okay" grin on my face, but I don't remember that. Initially, he wondered if I should have been taken to a more advanced hospital on Oahu. But after a few days, he saw that the care at Wilcox was great and I was in good hands.

I was wheeled to the room that would be my new home for the next six days. I was very, very tired and spent all day Friday trying to sleep. I say trying because all through the day and the night nurses kept coming in and doing things that woke me up: taking my temperature, fiddling with machines, checking my tubes and stuff. Late Friday my dad came into the room and quietly whispered that he was going home for the night and would get some clothes, take care of the dog, and be back in the morning. He tells me that he hardly slept that night, tossing and turning and running what happened over and over in his mind.

By Saturday morning, I was exhausted. (I really don't understand how they think you can actually rest in a hospital.) My dad showed up very early with bloodshot eyes. We were both dopey from lack of sleep, me more so because I was on some nerve pain killer medicine. My mom stayed by my side the whole time. My dad went out to deal with visitors and the ever-growing number of reporters who had heard what happened to me and were eager to break my story.

"I want to be the best surf photographer in the world," I told my dad. That was my way of saying, "Listen, I know my surfing days are over . . ." He just nodded, "I'm sure you will be," and tried to smile. He knew what it meant as well.

But by Saturday I changed my mind and started thinking about going surfing again. I was feeling better; my mind was less foggy, and there were so many people coming to see me and give me pep talks. Every time I would wake up and look around there were more balloons, more stuffed animals, and more flowers in the room. I remember it smelled great. But I also remember seeing a lot of sorrow on people's faces as they walked through the door of my hospital room—at least for the first minute or two. They wanted to see the same Bethany they had known before— and frankly, I looked pretty changed. So I quickly set them straight: I was the same person on the inside.

I put on a brave face for everyone, but I can't pretend it didn't get to me at times. I have this thought every second of my life: "Why me?" Not necessarily in a negative way—like "Why did this horrible thing have to happen to me?" But more "Why did God choose me and what does He have in mind for me?"

If I ever do start to get blue, I have my brothers to pull me back. They were laid back as always; they never let me know their horror or see their pain or fear. Timmy was always joking and Noah was my biggest protector. They were so strong, and that helped me be strong, too. I wasn't about to let my brothers show me up at anything!

The manager of the Radisson Hotel near the hospital called and gave my parents a room to use, so my dad would usually stay there at night and my mom would stay with me and then go and sleep there during the day. I remember on Saturday I started to feel a little bit of what they call phantom pain and it was very freaky. I could feel my arm, the arm that wasn't there! Your arm actually hurts, but you know there is nothing to hurt. This phantom pain still bothers me today.

My dad stayed with me on Saturday night. He said I was crying or whimpering like I was having a nightmare or something. I don't remember a thing.

Sunday came. We usually go to church on Sunday, but not that day. Lots of visitors came in the afternoon, so church came to us. The whole youth group from the Kauai Christian Fellowship and the North Shore Community Church showed up, prayed with me, and sang a bunch of worship songs I knew. That was pretty cool. There were so many of them that they spilled out of the room and into the hall.

All of this made me feel a bit more spunky—I was joking with friends, and really laughing, something I hadn't felt much like doing for a few days. Dr. Rovinsky would check me every day, usually in the morning. He explained that on Monday I would have another surgery that would take a flap of skin from under my armpit and swing it over, grafting it across the open wound. This would give the stub of my arm natural skin that would be held with stitches. Since I was already talking about going into the water, he made it clear that I had to wait until the stitches were taken out.

The doctor explained to us that I seemed to have a strong tolerance for pain and gave us all encouragement by saying, "The list of what Bethany will have to do differently is long; the list of what she will be unable to do is short." The doctors decided to give me blood transfusions as well because I was not replacing my own blood as quickly as they would have liked.

My dad, in particular, was afraid of transfusions because he had read about people getting AIDS or other diseases from tainted blood. But Dr. Rovinsky assured him that blood nowadays is screened. "If it was my daughter, I wouldn't hesitate," he told him. My dad knows how much the doctor loves his kids. "Okay," he said. "If that's how you feel, then I know it must be okay."

The next morning, a physical therapist came and I got out of bed and took a walk. I was really ready to do this; I was sick of lying in bed. I wish I could say I enjoyed being finally able to stretch my legs, but I had company the whole way, and I was dragging around bottles of liquid and medicine attached to a pole with wheels. It was kind of fun because I knew it was a sign of me getting better.

I had a visit from an occupational therapist,

too. She showed me how to tie shoes with one hand, put on and take off clothes, and other tips that I would need as soon as I got out of my hospital gown.

I was getting a little mischievous by then as well. A while ago my brother had brought me a realistic-looking fake foot when he came back from a trip to Mexico. It was a cool joke, so I had him bring it to the hospital. I stuck it under the sheet and when the nurse came in, I told her that I thought there was something wrong with my foot. "I don't know what's wrong," I moaned. "It doesn't feel so good . . ." You should have seen her face when she reached over and felt that cold rubber foot. I thought she would scream. Take that! This is what you get for waking me up all night! I also figured out how to turn off or fix the machines that I was hooked to when they started to buzz. With one, I just got up and unplugged it. Finally! A little peace and quiet.

When it came time for my surgery on Monday I was relieved. I just wanted to get things over with and get home. My family was with me as they wheeled me from my room to the hallway outside surgery. We all prayed together. I woke up back in my room with a fat bandage on my arm, still feeling groggy from the operation.

As soon as I was alert, my mom suggested that since the room had so many flowers and plants, we make it into a Garden of Eden. We put all the small plants into the bathroom and around the toilet, and the large plants and flowers in the main room. We even had flowers in the shower. When visitors came my mom would give them the tour of Eden.

On Tuesday I heard about a girl who was Timmy's classmate and who was in the hospital for seizures from a brain tumor, and decided to walk over and see her. We had a great visit, laughing and making jokes about our own situations. She was a Christian as well, so we both prayed together for each other. I brought her a whole bunch of flowers and balloons because I had way more than I would ever need. (And they kept on coming, too.)

I was getting antsy to leave—I wanted out of this twilight zone! I kept pestering my mom and dad: "When can I get outta here?" I pleaded. I was getting a little uncomfortable with all the attention, too. The hospital put security guards at my door to keep out uninvited visitors and the press.

Sometimes I was so tired of lying in bed that I would get up, grab some balloons, and walk around, bouncing them off my head. My brother even has a video shot of me doing this.

By Wednesday I was seriously stir-crazy. The doctor checked my wound again and said I could be released early. "Hooray!" I shouted. I felt like I was being sprung from jail! But then I was told that I could leave the hospital but I couldn't go home: there were dozens of reporters camped out on our lawn and I wouldn't be able to get any rest. So it was decided that we would sneak off to a friend's home in Anahola Beach.

I would have to stop at home to pick up some things. So we left the hospital that night through a back door and went home with a police escort. It was all too weird. When we got to the house, my dog was there and I cried for the first time. I was so happy to see her.

The next day a nurse came to change the dressing on my arm. This was the first time that any of us had seen just how much of my arm was missing. My grandmother went out on the porch and cried. It shook Timmy up so much that he went off to his room and stayed in bed all afternoon. And later on, he missed a lot of his senior year in school because he couldn't concentrate. "I want to be here if you need me," he told me. I really appreciated it; I know it set him back quite a bit and he had to fight hard to get his grades back up to speed later.

My parents had a rough time, too. Neither of them was able to work for almost three months, which put a big financial burden on our family. Fortunately the fees from the exclusive interviews we did on *20/20* and *Inside Edition* helped.

I thought I would be able to handle it okay. But when I looked at that little stump of an arm held together with long black stitches I almost fainted. "Oh my gosh," I thought. "I look like Frankenstein's monster." It was a lot worse than I had imagined. I was going to need help from someone much bigger than myself if I was ever going to get back in the water.

opening my eyes

We first met with blind psychologist Dr. Paul "Kai" Swigart at Wilcox Hospital on Sunday, November 4. Noah and Timmy were late—on purpose. They didn't think they needed to "see a shrink." So while we waited for the two of them, Kai felt his way into my room and found a seat near my bed.

I liked him immediately: he had a deep voice that was kind and reassuring. After I told him what I looked like, we talked about surfing, about my friends and hobbies, my church and family. Then I asked, "So have you always been blind?"

"No," he told me, "I could see until my early twenties when my degenerative condition took control."

"Is there a cure?"

"Possibly," he said. "There's an operation that could give me back my sight, but it's extremely expensive."

Just then I heard voices in the hall: my brothers had finally arrived. My family squeezed into my tiny hospital room and Kai began to retrace the events of that Halloween morning with each of us, one by one.

Then we talked about the future. I told Kai that a benefit was being planned to raise money for my prosthetic arm. And something suddenly dawned on me: "I'll never be able to have a real arm, but Kai might be able to get his sight back," I thought.

"I want you to use some of the money that

people are giving me to pay for your operation. I want you to see!" I told him.

"Thank you, Bethany," he said. "But I think that I am actually able to do more good being blind than I was able to being able to see. I *prefer* to stay this way."

I didn't understand it at first: why wouldn't he want to be able to see again? Why would he wish to remain with this handicap? But now I get it and I feel the same way. I think I may be able to do more good having one arm than when I had two. And it took Kai, a blind man, to open my eyes.

why I do it

People often ask me why I surf. I've tried to explain why I feel the way I do and it's impossible. Only surfers get it: the rush, the addiction, the way it stirs your heart, plays with your head, and tortures your body. Yet you keep coming back for more . . .

But let me try to paint a picture for you of what it's like to be in my shoes—or in this case, on my board:

Imagine straddling and balancing yourself on a foam board in the open ocean. You notice a rise in the sea, an oblong bump, coming rapidly toward you. You spin your board toward shore and dig your arms deep into the water, straining to pick up speed from a dead start. Sometimes it's agony. Concentrating on your paddling, you barely notice as the approaching wave gently lifts you up.

You keep on paddling, but now, as the wave brushes over the reef below, the gentle slope suddenly stands up straight and tall, and you feel the sudden pull of gravity. You and the board begin to drop down the vertical face of the wave.

This is it! One wrong move now and you will pitch head over heels with your surfboard into the trough of the wave, the place where all the energy and power of the throwing wave will be focused. No choice but to take it head on, so in one smooth move, you push up with your arms and swing your feet up underneath you. You are standing!

As you feel your board drop down the face of the wave, you suddenly realize that you are moving diagonally across a wave that is both going forward toward the beach and at the same time moving up and down. Yes! This is the dance you have worked so long and hard to do. But I don't think so much about it anymore, I just do it.

How long and how well can you do it? Much of that depends on your skill to turn, cut back, speed through fast-breaking sections, and slow down enough for the lip of the wave to throw completely over you, tucking you in a green cocoon for a moment before spitting you out into the clear (a maneuver called "getting tubed").

But as skilled as you are, sometimes nature is smarter, stronger, and tougher. The wave may suddenly take control and completely envelop you, dragging you to the bottom (we call that a "wipe-out" or "dirty lickings" in surfspeak).

There are other times, however, when nature is on your side. The wave, the conditions, and the dance all come together into an experience that penetrates you so deeply that you find yourself talking about that ride over and over again (so often that your nonsurfer friends moan, "Oh, no! Not again"). But all you want to do is relive it, to stay in that moment forever.

Some people ask me if it feels like when

you're on a roller coaster—the thrill and the fear and the flip-flop in your stomach. Yes, it does sometimes. But that's not even a fraction of what it's all about. It's not just adrenaline. Surfing is a force that moves you body and soul.

So this is why I do it. This is why I endure arms so sore and weak that they feel like wet noodles. This is why I swallow gallons of saltwater and get up at the crack of dawn day after day.

This is why I'm a surfer.

living in a world of what-ifs

"What about sharks?" That question is asked countless times to surfers, especially by those whose sports rarely take them near the ocean. The typical response is a half fatalistic, half que sera, sera: "Well, if your number is up . . ." Me? When I was asked, I'd usually just shrug and try not to think about it.

And truthfully, this isn't false courage. To

constantly dwell on what might happen would totally suck the joy out of the sport. Besides, it's like asking, "What if the roller coaster comes off the track? (It has happened.) What if the horse throws you? What if you get hit in the head with the baseball, the puck, or the golf ball? What if you crash on the bike, get run over while jogging, or break your neck in a fall while water skiing, climbing, or snowboarding, or get bitten by a rattler while hiking? See what I mean? Life is full of what-ifs. You can't let it hold you back. If you do, you're not really living at all . . . just kind of going through the motions with no meaning.

So you play it smart and take some precautions. Some surfers won't surf during dusk or dawn in places known to have an active shark population. Many prefer to have a buddy with them while surfing, as being the only bait out at a surf spot is just a little too creepy.

Any surfer who gets cut on a reef or from his surfboard fins is considered chumming for trouble and advised to get out of the water right away (sharks can smell blood and might be baited by it).

The fact is most surfers, even veteran surfers, have never seen a shark while in the water. But that doesn't mean they aren't there. Usually the animal darts by like a shadow sliding underneath the dangling legs of the surfer. Except in Hollywood movies like *Jaws*, it is *very* rare for sharks in the wild to knife through the water with their dorsal fin exposed. They prefer to move silently and stealthily underwater, a total surprise to their victims.

the history of surfing

The history of surfing is something surf nuts pride themselves on knowing: it's as important as, say, the *Mayflower* docking on Plymouth Rock. Here, in a nutshell, is Surfing's Story 101:

- Mark Twain tried surfing while on a visit to Hawaii in the 1800s. He found it much harder than it looked (the board went one way, Twain went another), and as surfers say, he "ate his lunch". . . and ended his lesson.

- The first Westerners to set eyes on the sport of surfing were the crew of the *Endeavor,* the ship that Captain Cook commanded. History tells us that the chiefs or "Alii" of Hawaii were renowned for their skills at surfing. Because early Hawaii had a strict caste system, keeping the nobles and commoners from mingling, the best surf spots and the best hardwood surfboards were the domain of the "kings." Some historians suggest that only the kings were permitted to stand erect on their boards while the rest of the surfing population had to be satisfied with riding prone.

- Songs and stories were told to celebrate the great surfers, and until horses arrived in the islands, the race track for gambling was centered around surfing contestants racing from one buoy to another while trying to knock their opponents off the wave.

- The first Caucasian to surf was a missionary in the 1800s enthusiastically trying out a koa wood board in the waves off tiny Nihau. Others surfed with their Hawaiian friends after their duties.

- In the early 1900s with the Kingdom of Hawaii now a territory of the United States, strong young Hawaiian watermen emerged who reinvigorated the sport. Led by Olympic swim star Duke Kahanamoku, Waikiki beach boy George Freeth, and with the help of famous writer Jack London, surfing became part of the new mystique of Hawaii. The sport blossomed again and soon was taking root in other ocean communities besides Hawaii.

- World War II put a temporary damper on the sport but at the same time exposed many young servicemen to the rolling waves of Waikiki. While the war slowed the growth of surfing, it was the technology coming out of the war effort that in the end helped to give the sport a new boost, as it led to the advent of lightweight surfboards. Surfboards became cheaper and more accessible to the average person.

- Eventually Hollywood discovered the sport, and using the theme of surfing in their music and films, created a media frenzy for anything surf-related, causing interest in the sport to skyrocket in the early '60s.

- Many of the older surfers resented the sudden influx of "kooks" and "gremmies"— names given to pretenders, beginners, or wannabes—as well as the crowding of their surf spots and the intrusion into their simple, relaxed lifestyle. Others saw business potential and decided to try to make a living by connecting themselves with the sport they loved.

- Young surfing moviemakers began to turn their cameras toward the ocean and created a series of documentary-style 16mm films, often with humorous narration, a few bikinis, and lots and lots of incredible surfing and breathtaking wipeouts. These low-budget projects would be taken from beach town to beach town, playing in rented halls or theaters for rowdy packed crowds of surfers.

- Surf contests, ratings, and point systems began to develop, as some in the sport saw the potential for surfing to gain the status of other professional sports. But for every young kid signing up to enter a contest, there was another youngster turning his back on professionalism, holding it as the antithesis of the heart and spirit of surfing. (A debate that continues to this day.)

- Clothing companies—often small surf-oriented families with a sewing machine—found themselves swamped with orders as the nation wanted to take on the look of the surf crowd. Some, like Hang Ten, Quiksilver, Rip Curl, and Ocean Pacific would become powerful business entities through the surfing culture.

- Progress in design and materials brought about the short-board revolution in the late '60s, opening the door of surfing to those who were intimidated by the weight and heft of long boards. And the resulting reduction in length and weight went a long way toward making the sport more inviting to women.

- Money began to lubricate the sport. Big sponsors stepped in to offer prize money for contests. Clothing and surf gear companies started paying talented young men (and eventually, a few women) to ride and compete for them.

- Surfers are pushing the extremes of the sport farther and farther to the place where only a handful of experts can handle the crazy-size surf that is being ridden.

keeping the faith

I believe in God.

I don't mean that I believe in Him like a person might believe in, say, gravity or the sun coming up in the morning. Those are just facts that don't mean anything. I mean I *really* believe in God.

Nobody made me believe; I don't think you can or should try to force someone to believe something. And even though my parents taught me stuff about God and read Bible stories (the story of Jonah, Christ walking on water, Noah's Ark, and the tale of the three brave Hebrews and the fiery furnace are my faves) to me from as early as I can remember. They also made sure that I was in church or Sunday school each week. But beyond that, it was my choice to become a believer in Him. The way I see it, putting your faith in God is something that each person has gotta come to on his or her own. It's your own personal relationship with Him; a bond that's as unique as a fingerprint.

Some people don't think much about this kind of stuff unless something terrible happens to them, or like my parents, until they are older. But I can remember putting my trust in Christ when I was just a little kid, probably around five years old. I know that's pretty rare—and some people might see it as a little weird. But I'm not embarrassed. Being tight with God is even more important to me than surfing.

When people ask me what my faith in Christ means to me, I usually answer in just one word: "everything!" This was true before the shark attack as well as after. And I truly believe that this faith is a big part of what did get me through it. It helps to know that even when you don't have a clue why something has happened in your life, someone up there has a master plan and is watching over you. It's a tremendous relief to be able to put your trust in God and take the burden off your shoulders.

My parents became Christians just a little while after they got married. They kept bumping into friends whose lives were completely changed for the better when they became believers. It got them interested, so they started reading the Bible and meeting with other Christians in their homes.

If you were to visit our house today, you would find a lot of evidence of our faith just lying around: music by Christian bands Zoe Girl, Relient K, and Cutlass; easy-to-read Bibles; even surf movies like *Changes* or *Specimen* produced by Christian surfers. We're proud of our faith—even though I know some people don't understand it or think we've gotten a little carried away in the whole religion thing. That's okay, because I don't think you ever have to explain or apologize for being a believer. It's the same as surfing: you can't know what it feels like, what it does for you, unless you're part of the club. All I can say is it gives me a really strong foundation for everything I do in life. It's like having a house built on solid rock.

my inspiration

I was once asked to name someone in history whom I admired a lot, someone I thought of as an inspiration or a role model. I had to think about it for a few minutes, because there are all kinds of people that I've learned about who are amazing. In fact, I could probably come up with a pretty long list. But I said "Father Damien."

Not many people know who Damien was or what he did, especially people outside Hawaii. I didn't know that much about him until I watched a video movie on his life just before my shark attack. To me, he's a role model of compassion.

His real name was Joseph Damien de Veuster, and he is one of Hawaii's most famous heroes. He was actually born in Belgium. Damien and his brother both became priests in the mid 1800s. It was Damien's brother who was supposed to go as a missionary to Hawaii but when he got too sick, Damien asked to go in his place.

During this time, leprosy was widespread on all the islands. It's a horrible disease: people lose the ability to feel the ends of their fingers and toes and so they often bang them or cut them without knowing, and this causes infection. The disease deforms people's faces as well. Doctors and officials, not knowing how to cure the disease, decided to force all those diagnosed with it to a remote section of the island of Molokai. Thousands of people were dumped at a place that was called a living graveyard. And there they just waited until their bodies were twisted and ruined by the disease that finally killed them.

Father Damien asked to be assigned to the leper colony at Kalaupapa, where, for sixteen years, he gave love and hope to all of those poor people. Damien eventually got leprosy himself and died, surrounded by his fellow lepers and friends.

That happened in 1889; Damien was only forty-nine years old. Damien sacrificed his life to help those who were suffering. He listened to God, fought for those who couldn't fight for themselves, and even gave up everything to serve others.

following in his footsteps

In my life I try to help by supporting, with my own money, a six-year-old girl in El Salvador named Dennis Vanesa Saltos. Even the smallest amount of money can make such a big difference. And I am working on plans to do other things to help kids who have limbs missing. I'd like to meet as many as I can and share with them my story, maybe help them work through all the fear and self-doubt. I've experienced it all firsthand, and I'm living proof that there's no such thing as a handicap—it's only in your head.

My church takes high school kids to work with poor people in Mexico every year. Now that

I am finally of high school age I *really* look forward to it. On the trip, we don't talk to the people much about God—hardly anyone speaks Spanish well enough anyhow. Instead, we *show* people our faith though our actions. So basically we try to help in any way we can.

Our kids, working with some people in San Diego called SPECTRUM Ministries, go over the border and into the back hills of Tijuana, where thousands of people live in little shacks without running water or sanitation. We set up portable bathhouses, and little kids line up by the hundreds to get a hot shower and a change of clean used clothing. We also distribute food and medicine and sometimes just play with kids in the local orphanages.

If I had to pick someone else I really admire who's actually around today? Okay, I admit it: I'd choose Mel Gibson. I have gotten to meet lots of famous people such as Oprah, Ellen DeGeneres, and Peter Jennings since my attack, but I'd love to have a conversation with Mel and tell him how much his movie *The Passion of the Christ,* meant to me. I saw the movie with my family when it first came out. I was moved to tears. Mel made this movie in spite of all the Hollywood people—and even some of his friends—telling him he was nuts. He didn't think he was wasting his time and money. He went ahead with it because of his faith in God. For this reason, Mel is kind of a missionary in his own way.

The way I see it, that's what a good missionary does: they spread the word of God through personal example. When I go to the mainland and talk about what happened to me, I always try to say something about my belief in God. I tell people, "God has a lot more to give and to offer than the world has to give. I am here today because of God, and I owe Him a lot." So maybe someone listening will be inspired to pick up a Bible or go to church and their lives will be better and richer as a result.

Things like that have happened already. I see that God is able to use my story to help others.

Once a girl (I never got her name) came up and told me that she had had cancer. When she saw my story it made her realize that she didn't need to give up; it made her want to fight hard too. She ended by saying, "Now I'm cancer-free."

I don't think I had anything to do with curing her of cancer—she did that herself. But if my story made her pledge to battle this disease and beat it with her own strength and willpower, than that would be enough for me.

The other day I got an e-mail telling me about another kid who lost his arm. He is an eighth grader from Raleigh, North Carolina, and he was very athletic like me, only his big sport was wake-boarding. He even had taken up guitar like I was doing before the attack. The lady who wrote me knew that Logan was pretty down, and she hoped that I might be able to cheer him up.

I grabbed the phone, called his house, and said "Hey, Logan, this is Bethany Hamilton from Kauai, Hawaii. You probably heard that I lost my arm to a shark."

"Yeah," he said softly.

"I just want you to know that I am surfing in the national finals with one arm," I told him.

"Yeah? Cool," he replied.

"Look, I know you may not feel great right now. I've been there. But I know that you can do a whole lot of stuff, too. You can and you will. Okay?"

Then we chatted some more, and I could feel his mood brightening. "Keep in touch and let me know what you're up to, okay?" I added. He promised he would, and I know that Logan is on the road back.

I felt great when I hung up the phone—and I think he did, too.

So I hope that kind of makes me a missionary. That would be cool, and I think both Mel and Damien would be stoked—and God would be proud, too.

an outpouring of aloha

Mike Wellman has this shop tucked away in the Waimea Valley of Kauai's west side. There he makes these beautiful surfboards—some of the most masterful I've ever seen. He runs his plane over the large foam surfboard and snowlike flakes of white foam spray in the air with each pass. It's the coolest thing. He is truly an artist.

Mike has probably made hundreds of surfboards, but there was one, he told me, that was different from all the others. It was made with aloha for a benefit in my name, and I know Mike poured his heart into it.

For those who make Hawaii their home, aloha means much more than a hello and good-bye greeting. It goes way back to the old Hawaiian traditions, and it means a mutual regard and affection of one person for another without any expectation of something in return. Translation: it means you do something from the pureness of your heart.

And it means love. Not just romantic love, but a self-sacrificial kind of love for others. Take the folks from my church: after we got home from resting up in Anahola, we discovered they had come into our house and radically cleaned the place, putting flowers everywhere. It just blew my mind. For two weeks, every night someone showed up with dinner. People kept stopping by offering to help out in any way they could.

I was also really moved by the number of people who wanted to help raise money for my family. At the time, nobody knew how much the hospital bills would be, or even with the health insurance, how much the portion my parents would have to pay. (Remember, my dad is a waiter and my mom cleans rental condos, so we don't exactly have a lot of bucks in the bank.) Also, people were trying to help get our family set up for any future expenses and the cost of the prosthetic arm. Guesses were that we might eventually need hundreds of thousands of dollars. And the cool thing is, people didn't ask us, they just looked at the situation we were in and said, "I want to help this family. They're gonna need it."

At the fundraiser, people donated over $75,000 to help with our expenses. Can you believe it? We couldn't. It sure made us feel humble and loved. Jill Smith organized the event and had no trouble getting residents of the island to pitch in. The Rip Curl Company dove right in, too, and helped spearhead the event.

On Saturday, November 15, only a few weeks after the attack, hundreds and hundreds of people (it was hard to count, as people came and went all afternoon) descended on the Marriot Grand Ballroom for a silent auction that included over five hundred items. There were works of art, clothing, and equipment donated from virtually every surf shop on the island, and they filled table after table in the vast hall.

Because I was still trying to build up my strength, it was decided that I wouldn't attend, which was kind of a bummer because I am the type of person who never likes to miss a fun party—especially one in my honor. Surf movies played nonstop on the huge screen, and shiny new surfboards, each inviting a high bid, lined the wall, including the one Mike had crafted, and one from the personal collection of world champ and Kauai neighbor Andy Irons. But the donations were not just surf-related. There was a case of fine wine, a music CD collection, a stay at the Princeville Resort, and massages by some of Kauai's professional masseurs.

The food was mostly what is called "light pupus," which I know sounds gross, but it is the Hawaiian word for finger food or small snack-type food. The people from Kauai Coffee came in and set up a stand selling different kinds of coffee drinks made from Kauai-grown coffee.

On a huge stage, some of the island's most sought-after names performed: Surf legend Titus

Kinimaka, Malani Bilyeu, Kanaloa, Tommy and Malia, and Revival, to name a few. Toward the end of the evening a special guest stepped onto the stage. Rock icon Graham Nash, formerly of the Hollies and the legendary Crosby, Stills and Nash, had come to perform on my behalf. My dad was floored: he told me he hadn't seen the island come together like this for a cause since the aftermath of Hurricane Iniki in 1992, which devastated all of Kauai. Who would have ever thought I would be as important as a natural disaster!

There was such an incredible mix of people at the benefit for Bethany Hamilton. Tan young surfers with T-shirts and shorts mingled with bankers, doctors, and real estate agents in their expensive aloha shirts and slacks. Surf beaters parked next to new Lexus SUVs in the parking lot. And the members of my Hanalei surf team were all there wearing their Friends of Bethany Hamilton T-shirts. They had a picture of me surfing and a gold hibiscus flower, a traditional symbol of

Hawaii, on them. More than two thousand of those T-shirts were printed, and all sold out in less than two hours.

The bidding was fast and furious: two guys started a bidding war over a surfboard, and it eventually went for two thousand dollars, the highest single bid of the night. It was unbelievable to think that all this money, all these people who came to this hotel that night, were here for me. I didn't even know a lot of them! And it made me really think, "Why me?" I mean, why should I deserve all this? But more than that, it made me think that if I get the chance to help somebody in the future, I, more than ever before, am really going to do it.

The folks from my church see how important it is to pay back to other people the kind of aloha and kindness that people, many of whom I didn't know, paid to me. And as uncomfortable and even embarrassing as it can get having people treat you like you are a serious charity case, the most important thing is to be so grateful and to do the same for somebody else when you get the opportunity.

the world sends get-well wishes

But that aloha spirit wasn't limited to Hawaii. All over America, even all over the world, people were reading news reports or magazine articles about me and were moved to write a note or a card, often slipping in cash, and mailing it off to the address that Noah had posted on my Web site. Children in classrooms sent me crayon drawings and get-well-soon wishes.

My folks, checking their mailbox, were astounded to find thousands of letters awaiting them. How could they possibly read all of them, much less respond? But they tried, finding good wishes—along with checks or cash, sometimes hundreds of dollars, sometimes a five dollar bill— in the envelopes. All of us were stunned by what was happening. We could understand the aloha that was given to us on Kauai—that's what we would have done if this had happened to anyone we knew. But for all this kindness to come from people who had heard about my story from the media? Well, we were shocked.

In talks around the dinner table we discussed why this might be happening. I'm a big believer that most people in this world are truly kind, generous, and bighearted, and this supports my theory. I think they heard about this kid who got her arm bitten off and they wanted to simply help out in some small way. My mom's theory is that there are a lot of people who have a deep faith in God and they wanted to encourage me because I was outspoken about my faith. Dad's take on it? He thinks many people let their problems get them down and walk around with this "Woe is me" attitude. Well, here I come, determined to get back the life that the shark tried to take from me. No woe—just go, go, go! Maybe I gave them the kick they needed to get back on their feet. In the end, we really don't know why so many people wrote, prayed, or gave, but we are very, very grateful for each one of them and their thoughtfulness.

One organization, Save Our Seas, heard about what had happened to me and heard me say in an interview that if I couldn't surf again, maybe I would take surf pictures. So they offered to train me in video and still photography as well as get me scuba-certified and enrolled in a special course for underwater photography. It was an awesome offer that I still might take them up on when I get a little less busy.

For now, I'm just taking things one day at a time. My mom started to keep a big scrapbook with all the articles that were being printed about me. Most of them were pretty accurate and got the basic facts right. Some of the longer articles in magazines actually gave a better picture of all that was going on. A few years from now it will be fun to pull out that scrapbook and read it. Right now, well, we are still adding pages.

12

on being kind
of famous

My first indication that my life would never be the same again came just as we were leaving the hospital. Instead of going out the main entrance, we had to go through this maze of hallways and sneak out a back door.

There were hospital security guards with us, and when we got to our car, there were two Kauai policemen who followed us to a house in Anahola where I could continue to recover in privacy.

My parents explained to me that there was a mob of TV people eagerly waiting to shove microphones in my face. Mom in particular didn't like this intrusion into our lives: she just wanted me to get better and not be burdened with a million questions. She was being a mom, protecting her daughter. And honestly, I really don't enjoy being in the spotlight. It's a really strange feeling, kind of like living in a fishbowl.

Nowadays, everywhere I go people call my name or come up to me. I'm a celebrity of sorts, but I don't feel very comfortable with it, even though I made the choice to put myself out there. I could have kept quiet after the attack and no one would be watching me on TV. Sometimes you make a choice and you don't understand exactly everything that goes with it.

This choice is what happened when, sitting with my family and a few close friends at the beach house in Anahola, I decided that I would be willing to go on TV and tell my story; especially if I could be free to talk about how my faith in Christ has helped me. At the time, things were happening very fast: I was more or less being myself in the few interviews that I gave, and that included expressing my belief that God has a plan for me. My mom was a little worried that the media exposure might be too much to handle, not just for me but for all of us. "I'm okay with doing interviews if you guys think that God can use me," I told her.

My parents pretty much left the decision up to me. If I had wanted to just hide out, they would have been okay with that. And even now, I think that if I decided that I don't ever want to do another interview again in my whole life they would be fine with that too. Coming to this decision was pretty easy—of course I had no idea what I was getting myself into!

Here's the thing: a shark story fascinates people. I have to admit, before I was attacked, I liked to watch programs about sharks and all the *Jaws* movies. (I don't anymore.) People tend to ask me the same kinds of questions: "Did it hurt?" (Not really.) "What were you thinking?" (Get to the beach, quick!) "Did you see the shark?" (Not very well.) And most of all, "Aren't you afraid to go back in the water?" (Not really, but every once in a while I get creeped out.) I try not to make a big soap opera out of the shark attack. I would rather focus on what God has allowed me to do in picking up the pieces of my old life and adjusting to parts that are new and different for me. Most of all, I want to use my story as a way to tell people about God's story. It seems like He has given me the attention of the world for a moment and I had better take advantage of it while I can.

I get stacks and stacks of mail—when the story first broke in the news I would gets hundreds of letters a week! I try to read as many of the letters as I can, but there is no way I could ever write back. I would be busy 24/7 just doing that.

But as my family and I talked about the opportunities for me to tell people about my faith, we decided we needed help coping with all the media craziness that was sure to follow. So we called some of our friends from Kauai who were agents and asked them to be our guide and our buffer.

The first TV show that I was on was *20/20*. Whoa! Pretty major. It took hours and hours of film, and all that was on television was about ten minutes of stuff. Chris Cuomo was the guy who flew over to interview me and ask me all kinds of questions: Where were you? What were you doing? How did it feel? Were you scared? And a whole bunch more, so many, that to be honest, I started to get annoyed. I felt like I was being interrogated!

After that, I had lots of phone interviews and told my story a million times (or at least it felt like that). By the second week of November I had been interviewed by *Inside Edition, Life Magazine, Sports Illustrated, The Early Show, Good Morning America, The Today Show,* and *CNN Live.* I was everyone's favorite interviewee. Pretty much everyone asked the same things, so I got pretty good at telling my story. Just one problem: it started to get a little boring and even at times frustrating, because I was so sick of talking about me!

Not every interview was torture. One "phoner" I did was with a guy who won the Pipeline Masters contest a long time ago. His name is Joey Buran, and he still surfs but is also a pastor in California. It was cool talking to him, because in a lot of ways he really understood me. I think that's the biggest problem with these reporters: they have a hard time asking the right questions because they don't really get what I do or why I do it. So even if they do all their homework, it's still really hard for them to relate to me or me to them. It's like we're talking two different languages.

do celebs ever get to sleep?

A few months after my attack I went traveling around doing interviews on television shows. I was on a show in Los Angeles and then went flying off to do a whole bunch more in New York City. We arrived around 10 PM, and I wasn't feeling good the whole time. I had a pretty high fever. Everyone who went with me got sick too. We landed at JFK airport during a snowstorm. The airport was filled with angry people who had been grounded by the blizzard or who couldn't get a taxi to their destination. Me? I had never seen snow before so I was really psyched!

We decided to visit relatives in New Jersey so we rented a car and started driving south. Along the way we pulled off at a restaurant. It was snowing like crazy, and my dad started heaving snowballs at me, which wasn't fair because I didn't know how to make them with only one hand (it didn't take me long to figure it out though). I think he did it to give me the challenge. He knows I never back down from a challenge!

When we got to New York City, I went from one interview to the next. I was a guest on MTV announcing what videos were coming up next. I read what I was supposed to say off a big sign someone was holding. I hope I didn't come off sounding dumb!

At the hotel, they pick you up to take you to the television show in a limousine. People think that a limo is a really cool kind of car but now that I have been in them, I think they're way too showy. Honestly, I prefer my old Beater back home to a stretch any day!

I had never been in a TV studio before. They all have a "green room," which cracks me up because nine out of ten times it's not really green (so why do they call it that, would someone tell me?). These are places where guests on TV shows wait until they are called. The rooms are usually full of food and drinks (anything and everything you could imagine) plus a TV to watch the show in progress.

The whole TV studio process is kind of interesting. When you watch TV, you only see the host and their guests, but in reality there are lots and lots of people all around. Some shows with audiences even have signs that tell the people when to clap. At first it's very nerve-racking to have all these big cameras pointing at you: they do your hair and makeup; then you get out there, and they shine big lights on you and hang a microphone over your head. At first I was totally distracted. But after a few times, I got used to it. You kind of have to tune it all out and just focus on the conversation and the questions being hurled at you.

A director makes sure that everything runs on time, and the host is getting signals about how much time is left but is able to coolly keep a conversation going without freaking out as the clock ticks down.

Some TV shows are taped, edited, and then run at a later date. In this case (like when I was on *20/20* and *Inside Edition*) they film a whole bunch of stuff but only show a tiny bit. They don't ask you what to leave in or take out—so you kind of cross your fingers and hope for the best.

When my friends ask me what the best thing about going to New York was, I always say there were two things that stand out for me:

1. The snow and everything that goes with it; ice skating and making snowmen and throwing snowballs.
2. The free all-you-could-drink sweet wild orange tea they gave me at the Sheraton Towers.

That's it.

I guess you could say I wasn't all that impressed by the big city. There are lots of homeless people in New York, and that made me really sad. The guys at MTV had me go on some kind of spending spree but there wasn't really anything that I was interested in buying at the overpriced shops there. So while we were doing this, I passed a lady sitting on a steaming sewer grate to keep warm. I felt sorry for her and tried to help by giving her some of our lunch and a little bit of money. The people I was with acted like it was some kind of big deal. It's not. I think that it's simply what Jesus meant when he said "When you do good things to the least of these you do it to me." It amazes me that so many people in New York can just walk by a stranger who is cold and sick on the street and not even look them in the eye. I can't do that. I can't turn away from someone in need. Not when just a little kindness can go so far.

I'm on Oprah!

A lot of people were nice to us. Peter Jennings let my whole family hang out in his office even though I didn't do an interview with him. From New York I went to Canada and Chicago to be on Oprah's show. Like most of the TV people who interviewed me, she was nice and kind, but it's not like these people want to hang out with you after the show and get an ice-cream sundae. It's more of a hello-good-bye type of thing. But I didn't really have any expectations so I wasn't disappointed.

It never occurred to me at the time, but when you go on all these TV shows there are millions of people who are watching you at home, and they suddenly feel like you have just come into their house and they know you. You're an instant celebrity, just like that.

For me the whole thing about being recognized, being "famous," is both a blessing and a curse. I like that my life can serve as encouragement to people; I like that I can tell people about

Christ. Then there are the negatives: all the activity and attention gets in the way of my being able to do things that I want to do. For example, if I just want to go out and be with my friends, it becomes hard when strangers come up and want to meet me. I feel like I have to be nice to them, but to be honest, sometimes I just want to ignore them.

Doing interviews cuts into my being able to go to surf contests or camp with my church or hang out with my friends. I even got way behind on my schoolwork because of all the things I was doing and had to cram and work really hard to catch up.

I know that God has put me in a place where I have a chance to be of help to people all over the world. And I constantly have to remind myself, ten times a day (if not, my brothers remind me, my parents remind me) that this isn't just about me being in the spotlight. There's a greater good here, so if that means I have to make a few sacrifices or give a gazillion interviews, then it's worth it.

no autographs, please!

Sarah Hill and I were given first-class seats on the six-hour flight from Kauai to L.A. It's pretty brutal being cooped up on a plane that long, and we hardly slept a wink. But we made the trip because I had been invited to give out Dove awards at the Gospel Music Association; the Grammys for Christian music. I was psyched.

Sarah suddenly elbowed me in the ribs. "Hey! Patrick Swayze is sitting right near us," she whispered. "He keeps glancing at you. I think he knows who you are." That made me laugh out loud. Patrick Swayze knows *me?*

"He keeps looking back at you!" she insisted. "You want me to give you a piece of paper and pen; you could ask for his autograph?"

"No," I replied.

"Why not?" Sarah asked anxiously.

"'Cause I get tired of people asking me for my autograph." I told her.

It's not easy being a celebrity. And I'm not sure I'm very good at it. When I watch my interviews, I notice that I hem, haw, fidget, and give back a blank stare or one-word responses a lot of the time. Sometimes I'm just not in the mood to talk. And often I'm just plain bored telling the same story over and over again.

But I'm trying to get used to the whispers and stares that come not from just being a girl with one arm but being *the* girl shark-attack victim.

People aren't always nice. While I was waiting with Sarah for a flight, a man approached me and in a cocky and cruel way asked, "So, are you still surfing Tunnels?"

I couldn't help it. I felt my eyes well up with tears. "What was *that* supposed to mean?" I asked Sarah, who gave the guy a full dose of what Hawaiians call "stink eye." "Forget it," she told me. But that's easier said than done. Sticks and stones *and* cruel words do hurt me.

Strangers approach me on the beach, in

airports, in shops and restaurants. They ask for autographs; they come up and tell me I'm "an inspiration." I'm interrupted at dinner by people wanting to be in a photo with me. It's totally bizarre.

And you know what's even stranger? Being a top professional surfer would have brought me only a sliver of this recognition and probably only within the tight-knit surfing community. "You're something more now than a surfer," friends tell me. "You're the bearer of hope for those who have been handed a bad deal in the card game of life." And you know what? That's a lot of responsibility for anyone to take on!

Luckily, I have my home base to keep my head on straight. I don't get any VIP treatment in my little corner of the world and that's how I like it! To my friends and family I'm just Bethany, and nothing much has changed in spite of the loss of an arm and the media frenzy.

This is the *real* world, where people love

and care about each other, warts and all. I really hope Patrick Swayze is lucky to have his own home team who feels the same way about him.

back in the waves

Imagine the one thing you love to do the most. Now imagine, out of nowhere, something happens and you realize you may never be able to do it again. How do you feel? Sad? Angry? Shell-shocked? For me, the answer was all of the above.

In the hospital, I would look over at the bandaged stump where my arm used to be and think, "Now what?" For a while, I doubted that I would ever surf again. Everybody knows that it takes two arms in order to surf. I tried to tell myself, "Hey, I'm okay with this. I mean, surfing isn't everything, right? You'll find something else to do to have fun." I remember telling Sarah, "I guess I'll have to get back into soccer." And I told my dad I wanted to be a surf photographer, since that would be the only way I could still stay close to the sport if I couldn't directly participate in it.

I know that a lot of my friends and my parents' friends privately thought that my days as a stand-up surfer were over. They were kind enough to never say that to me but I know that they were thinking it.

Only my brother Timmy knew nothing could keep me out of the water. He figured that I would join him in being a body boarder, since they don't stand up on a wave. He even had his sponsor, Viper, send me a free pair of body board fins.

But even before I got out of the hospital—in fact, by the second day of my one-week stay—I was talking differently about the possibility of surfing again. My whole family stood behind me and tried to encourage me as much as possible.

My parents had no doubt that I probably could figure out a way to get up on a board but I know they felt my competitive days were over. "Bethany, I am sure you can do whatever you put your mind to," my dad told me. He was a great coach, the king of the pep talk. I would hear his words echoing in my ears every time I got on my board.

Some people thought that I might be afraid to go back in the ocean ever again. But to be honest, I didn't really have any fear of that. I had about three to four weeks of healing and recovery before I could give surfing with one arm a try. I had some stitches on what was left of my arm that had to come out, and the doctor ordered me to stay out of the water until everything healed up. I set a deadline for myself: Thanksgiving Day.

The day before Thanksgiving, some of my friends from the Hanalei Surf Company girls' team were going to go surfing. I decided I would go down to the beach and just watch . . . but of course, I couldn't stand just to do that. The water, the breeze, it was all too tempting.

the first surf

The wind on Kauai usually blows from the northeast. These are called tradewinds, but on that day it was coming from a different direction. This makes all the surf spots that are typically good with tradewinds become choppy, blown out, and terrible, yet opens up surf spots that usually don't get surfed because the wind is not right for them.

In addition to the unusual wind pattern, we had a decent northeast swell, so with the wind conditions and the swell directions, we all knew that a little secret place in Kilauea would be the spot.

The beach we chose is off the beaten path. We all knew that this first surf session since the attack, for better or worse, would be a very important moment—and would surely make the news. We drove to the beach late in the afternoon, and when we came down the trail, what we saw got all of us really pumped up. The place was about as good as it ever gets. Sand bars had formed all over the surfing area and it was packed with local talent.

I decided to ride a long board, my nine-foot one, instead of a short board, because with a longer board a wave is much easier to catch and the board is more stable. The more advantage I could give myself to start with, the better. I told myself, "You can do it. You can paddle and get up with one arm." But quickly another voice inside my head yelled back, "Forget it. You're going to fail." I tuned out that nagging self-doubt and headed for the water.

My brother Noah wanted to film the ride on his video camera, so he put it in an underwater housing and swam out with it. (He is so stoked about my first ride that he carries it around on his laptop and shows people all the time.)

My dad took off work and came into the water for a front-row view, just swimming along with me and shouting, "Go, girl!" at the top of his lungs, and hooting with encouragement. A family friend named Matt George, a writer for *Surfer* magazine, was with us at the time, so he came down and was cheering me on. And of course Alana and a bunch of my friends were there too.

Alana and I walked into the surf together just like we did on that early Halloween morning. It felt so good to step into the liquid warmth and taste the salty water that swept over me. It was like coming back home after a long, long trip. To think I had come so close to losing all these things that I loved so much forever: the ocean, my family, and my friends. I was not afraid of being attacked by a shark. I didn't even think about it. My whole mind was concentrated on catching a wave and getting up on my feet. After that, what to do next would come naturally.

Alana paddled through the rolling white water (surfers call this "soup") and headed farther out to the blue unbroken waves. I decided to make it easy on myself and ride some soup to begin with. In some ways it was like learning to surf all over again. I had to learn how to paddle evenly with one arm, and when I felt the wave pick me up, I had to put my hand flat on the center of the deck to get to my feet rather than grabbing the surfboard rail the way you would if you had two hands.

My first couple of tries didn't work: I couldn't get up. I have to admit I was a little bit discouraged. I thought it was going to be easier than it was. My dad, who was in the water with me, kept shouting, "Bethany, try it one more time. This one will be it!" So I did.

Then it happened. A wave rolled through, I caught it, put my hand on the deck to push up and I was standing. I guess I started getting the technique wired after that. Of course once I was on my feet, everything was easy.

It's hard for me to describe the joy I felt after I stood up and rode a wave in for the first time after the attack. I was incredibly thankful and happy inside. The tiny bit of doubt that would sometimes tell me "You'll never surf again" was gone in one wave! Even though I was all wet, I felt tears of happiness trickling down my face.

Everyone was cheering for me. It was a great

moment! I caught a whole bunch of waves that day, mostly white water, but getting up got easier and easier each time.

The next day, Thanksgiving, we were supposed to be leaving for the mainland. I went down to the beach that morning with Sarah and my friends. I wasn't suppose to go surfing but I couldn't control myself.

I saw a guy with a nice camera on the beach, and I was afraid he might be a paparazzo, so I walked up to him and asked him to please not take any pictures of me surfing. Then I paddled out with my friends.

Holt got out his video camera and filmed my rides. That day I didn't ride the soup but took off on the blue waves. It was much easier than it was the first day.

When I got home and told my parents that I couldn't restrain myself and that I went surfing, they weren't upset. In fact, they understood completely . . . because they were surfers too. As time went on, I got more and more comfortable catching waves and standing up with one arm. I figured out some things I could do to help as well. Getting out through powerful surf was going to be hard because most surfers grab the rails of their boards with both hands and dive the nose under oncoming white water, a move called "duck diving," since it resembles what a duck does when it goes underwater. I couldn't duck dive with one hand until we came up with the idea of putting a hand strap in the top center of my board that I could grab hold of and use to push under the white water.

Sometimes people ask me if I am ever scared of sharks now that I am surfing all the time again. Well, the answer is yes, sometimes my heart pounds when I see a shadow under the water. I do think about it a whole lot more than I ever did before I was attacked. Sometimes I have nightmares about being attacked by a shark. And I am not ready to go out and surf Tunnels again and am not sure I will ever go back there.

Alana and I sometimes talk about it. Sometimes we say to each other that we will go out there again on October 31—a year from the day I got attacked, just to prove to ourselves that we are not afraid. But then I get spooked.

Yet even when my nerves get the best of me, I do know this: God is watching out for me, and while I don't want to do something stupid like paddling out where someone has just seen a shark, in the end, I trust Him to take care of me.

the best I can be

I wish I could say I just hop on a board and that's all it takes to win a competition. The truth is a lot of stuff—and a lot of sweat—goes into preparing, now more than ever, because of my attack and because of the level of competition I've reached.

So here's my typical daily "Rocky" routine:

I run on the beach, swim laps, lift dumbbells, do lots of stretches and stomach crunches, and ride an indo board (aka a balance board) and a skateboard. There are times when the last thing I feel like doing is running another mile, but I am seriously concentrating these days on stepping up the physical. So just in case I don't feel like pushing myself, I have a great coach from Australia, Russell Lewis, who has trained other world champs, to push me farther and harder than I ever think I (or any human!) can go. He's been with me four years and he's amazing. He helps you feel totally prepared: once, he had half the girls he was training fill out heat sheets and pretend they were judging a surfing contest while the others went surfing (and then we switched roles). The goal: to help the girls in the water learn what judges were looking for. Russell critiqued us on our riding style, performance, even head placement (the head is the heaviest part of the body, and putting it in the right place makes a difference in drive and speed down a wave).

I have another coach, Ben Aipa, the legendary coach of surfing gods like Sonnny Garcia and Kelly Slater, who has helped me a lot since the attack. I have to do things differently now, and Ben has a solution to every problem. For example, he taught me to kick with my feet while paddling (with only one arm, you don't have lot of power to propel yourself). Well, I was kicking, but I just didn't seem to be up to speed. So he said, "Don't be afraid to grunt and make noise out there!" I felt pretty stupid at first, but I did it, and it worked. Anything he comes up with I listen to.

My other coaches are my parents. Dad's my game plan man. Before a heat, we sit and watch the waves coming into shore, and then we discuss my best approach. My mom coaches me more on the mental and spiritual side of my surfing. She kind of helps me get into my zone. We pray for my peace of mind out there.

surfspeak

One of the coolest things about surfing is it has a language all its own. Here are just a few of the terms we surfers use in and out of the waves:

Glassy: When the surface of the water is smooth and without wind

Set: Waves usually come in sets of two to five

Angry growler: A huge, gnarly wave

Haired out: Too scared to take off on a wave

Power turn: A manner of surfing where each turn is taken with strong, deliberate force

Scorched: Being dropped in on or burned by another surfer. Sometimes refers to taking a severe wipeout

Promising swell: A swell predicted by the weather service that is starting to show up

Stoked: More than excited

Paddling out: Stroking out to where the waves begin to break

Jostling for position: A term used in competitive surfing for getting into the place where you can catch the wave first

Drop in: Sliding into a wave

Aerials: A maneuver that has a surfer soaring in the air before landing

Backdoor barrel: Dropping into a wave so late that you have to go through the pitching peak to get to the shoulder of the wave.

Grommet (Grom): A young surfer

Thruster: A three-finned board

Ding: A dent on a board

Tiki: A wooden god formerly worshipped by Polynesians

Duck dive: Diving under waves to get to the sets

Groovemeister: A Kauai term for someone who is smooth when surfing

Close out: When the wave breaks all at the same time, giving you no place to go

Rip: The current that draws a swimmer out to sea; also, the art of aggressive surfing

Off the wall: A surf spot on Oahu that attracts lots of photographers

Being pitched: To be thrown off the top of the wave

Airdrop: A very late takeoff when the surfer drops through the air to the bottom of the wave

Wax up: To put sticky wax on top of the surfboard to keep from slipping

Boil: A bubbling movement of water around a submerged rock or reef head

Chop: Small waves on the face of the water or a wave produced by unfavorable winds

Pummeled: Getting tossed around by a breaking wave

Aggro: Aggressive surfing or surfer

Inside the bowl: The bowl refers to a part of some waves that tend to wrap around into a bowl shape

Ankle slappers: Small waves

Bottom turn: the turn made at the bottom of a breaking wave

Cutback: A sharp turn back toward the power center of the wave

Goofy foot: Right foot forward

Regular foot: Left foot forward

Kick out: To thrust out of the wave at the end of the ride

Bail: To abandon the board and head for the bottom

Bogus: Fake

Carve: To surf using lots of turns and cutbacks

Full on: Committed and intense

Gnarly: Heavy, powerful, thick

Gun: Big board used for giant surf

Impact zone: The place where all the power of a breaking wave focuses

Line up: The place where waves first start to break and where surfers sit

Macking: Huge sets like a Mack truck

Quad: Four fins

Getting worked: Taking a bad wipeout

Kook: A novice surfer who gets in the way

Dirty lickings: To take a severe wipeout

Rag dolled: To be held under and swept around by the power of the wave

Skeg: The fin of a surfboard

Soul Surfer: A surfer who merely surfs for the love of the sport

Spongers: Surfers who ride body boards

Soup: The white water made by a breaking wave

Stringer: The wooden strip running down the center of a surfboard

Flat: No surf

Off shore: The preferable wind direction blowing from land to sea

Zoo: A place packed with surfers

Burned: When another surfer takes off on the same wave that you are riding

Stuffed: When a surfer burns you and then by his actions forces the wave to bury you

Tubed: Riding deep inside the pitching wave

14

aftermath

I think a lot about how my accident has affected the lives of the people around me. When something like this happens, you're not the only one who feels pain and suffering. You're not the only one who is left with a scar.

Alana is normally a kind of quiet girl and I know she tends to keep a lot inside. I know that she's had a hard time with this—there were nights she was so haunted by what happened that she was too scared to sleep alone in her room. Instead, she would crawl into her parents' bed. She'd also cry—for no reason in particular. And I do think that it's also had an impact on her surfing. She doesn't like to surf some of the fine breaks that are far from shore, and she has never been able to bring herself to return to Tunnels.

We talk about it off and on and both feel the same way, even though I am the one who was actually attacked. Alana never even saw the shark, but being so close to a terrible accident can have the same affect as being the victim. She knows that it could have just as easily been her.

We have been friends since *"hanabata* days" (Hawaiian term used for the days of childhood but it really means from the days we had snotty noses), and we are more like sisters than friends. And to have something bad happen to your sister really hits you deeply.

I don't really push her to talk about it. With our friendship, there's this kind of unspoken language between us. I can almost read her mind and she can read mine, so we don't have to spend a lot of time with words. We get it. We understand what the other is feeling without asking, "What's up?"

Alana's dad, Holt, also has a lot to deal with. He's constantly asking himself, "What if the ambulance hadn't come in time? What if I had made the decision earlier that morning that the waves were too small to bother with and we all had gone home? What if the bite had been more severe?" Alana, her family, and I have all had counseling to help us deal with the stress. That counseling seemed to help a lot. Today, I can honestly say it's not something I constantly think about—which is a major step toward healing. Of course, every once in a while I see myself in the mirror and it hits me: "Whoa, you only have one arm, girl!" And every so often I see pictures of myself with both arms and I feel a twinge of sadness. But I'm working—we all are—to get over it. To deal with the new challenges. Past is past. On to bigger and better!

the new me

The changes I've undergone have been both physical and emotional. First of all, I don't wear shoes much anymore (*you* try tying your laces with one hand!). I either go barefoot or wear my rubber slippers. I have a prosthetic arm, but honestly, I never wear it. It just hangs by the window in my room. I tried it, but it was too unnatural and restricting with all the straps and the clothing that must go over it, especially for someone like me who spends 90 percent of her day in a bathing suit. So I just kind of run around with my one arm—I call what's left of the other "stumpy."

I have an agent, Roy, in Beverly Hills trying to find deals for me. He wants to help get my story out all over the place, to use it to inspire people. He also wants me not to have to worry about the future. But it's a funny kind of relationship because I want to do all the interviews and other things he lines up, but at the same time I'm always trying to get out of them. Things like interviews keep me from doing what I love: surfing.

I worried that Rip Curl wouldn't want to sponsor me after the attack, but they were incredibly supportive. They just want me to be myself.

Of course if I enter and win contests, that makes them really happy, and naturally they want me to wear Rip Curl clothing (which I like to do because I think it's cute). They think it's funny that I knot up one sleeve of their shirt when I am doing a TV interview. Right from the start, while I was still in the hospital, they let me know that they were sticking with me. And that is a very cool thing for a company to do. Now, besides winning contests, they see me as an ambassador of goodwill and the surfing culture. If I ever stop entering contests I am sure that I will still be sponsored to surf and that I will be in ads featuring their clothing.

And here is the coolest thing: if I never win another contest, or if I decided to leave the contest scene altogether, people would still know me and recognize me as "that surfer girl who got her arm bitten off by a shark." I think I'll forever be tied to the sport because of what happened, which is very cool. I'd like people to associate me with surfing, even when I'm ninety years old! I have a feeling I'll be on a board even then.

What's in my bag when I travel:

- Bible
- lip balm with sunscreen
- Rip Curl clothes
- no cell phone. . . . not healthy!
- no shoes!
- my fave CDs for the flight or drive
- surf magazines (I read the ones I'm in, but I think I sound like a goof a lot of the time)
- a camera to shoot pics to show my friends and family back home
- a cool journal to keep track of what I am doing and feeling
- surfboard

me in the movies?

Roy promised me there would be some really big things coming up for me. But a movie of my life? I can't really imagine it (who will play me?) but I am looking forward to the surfing scenes, which I will do, and I have faith that it will be a true movie and convey my faith. I guess I've even had a little taste of the Hollywood scene already: I've been on the red carpet at the ESPY and Teen Choice Awards. Who would ever have thought I'd be meeting Britney Spears and rubbing elbows with celebs? It was wild—and I had my friends Chantilly and Tiffany from Beverly Hills to escort me to these events and style me. Thank God— without them, I would have probably been walking down the red carpet barefoot!

I was just in Portugal, where I made a short film for Volvo. In it, I drive a car down the beach and teach surfing to Grete Consuela, the jockey. It was fun, although I don't really think I have it in me to be an actress. It took way too long—almost a whole day—to shoot just one little three-minute commercial. Actors must have a lot of patience.

I'll be back in New York City in the winter for an event at the Waldorf-Astoria Hotel. I'll be receiving an honor from the Women's Sports Federation. I am very determined to do a lot of cool surfing before that award to prove I deserve it.

All of this glamorous stuff is great, but my biggest excitement is getting to work with the World Vision Foundation, which is a Christian humanitarian organization that helps poor children in about a hundred countries around the world. I'm excited to work with World Vision because through them I can use my voice to help children living in poverty with disabilities get the care and support they need. Many children around the world have to fend for themselves if they have disabilities or health problems. World Vision has a program called Put Hope in Motion that lets me use my surfing to raise awareness and funds to help these kids.

part of a plan

When I was a kid I learned something that Christ said. As a person who lives near the beach, it made a lot of sense to me:

> These words I speak to you are not incidental additions to your life, homeowner improvements to your standard of living. They are foundational words, words to build a life on. If you work these words into your life, you are like a smart carpenter who built his house on solid rock. Rain poured down, the river flooded, a tornado hit—but nothing moved that house. It was fixed to the rock.
>
> But if you just use my words in Bible studies and don't work them into your life, you are like a stupid carpenter who

built his house on the sandy beach. When
a storm rolled in and the waves came up,
it collapsed like a house of cards."
— MATTHEW 7:24-27 (THE MESSAGE)

My plans to be a professional surfer got hit pretty
hard on that Halloween morning. It was my own
personal tornado. In the days, weeks, and months
that followed I had a lot of cleaning up to do. Often, it was scary or trying. And I won't lie to you:
in some ways it still is.

But for me, knowing that God loves me and
that He has a plan for my life that no shark can
take away is like having solid rock underneath me.
Look, lots of bad stuff happens to people. That's
life. And here's my advice: don't put all your hope
and faith into something that could suddenly and
easily disappear. And honestly, that's almost anything. The only thing that will never go away, that
will never fail you, is your faith in God.

I have been very blessed in my life. People
ask me, "How can you say that after this horrible

thing happened to you?" Because I have to look at the big picture: I have a family that loves me, supports me, and encourages me to go after my dreams. I have a big *ohana* of Christian friends and friends from the community and the surf world that care about me. I have close personal friends, like Sarah, Holt, Troy and Malia, Alana, Kayla, Noelani, Savana, Kristen, Michelle, Camille, Jackie, Kalie, Kyah and Summer—to name a few. These people like me for who I am: one arm, two arms or no arms, it doesn't matter.

But most of all, I have a relationship with Christ that keeps me strong and helps me see how good can come out of a bad situation. I think the reason I haven't gotten all bummed out about losing an arm is due to God. I think that the reason I have been able to tell my story on TV and in magazines is because God wanted other people to know that He is the rock that you can build your life on.

So I think this was God's plan for me all along. I am not saying that God *made* the shark bite me. I think He knew it would happen, and He made a way for my life to be happy and meaning-ful *in spite* of it happening. I know that sometimes people get angry at God when bad things that can't be explained happen to them. Which I can understand, and I know that I sometimes wonder, "Why me?"

There was this guy named Job in the Old Testament who was a believer but had really terri-ble things happen to him. So bad that his friends told him that he must have done something really awful to deserve what was happening, and that he ought to just cuss out God and die. His reply to those guys was "Even if God kills me, yet I will trust Him."

He knew that God was good and that he loved him in spite of everything. Well, I can't ex-plain why, but I have the same kind of attitude. I know in the beginning my family struggled to make sense of my attack, but now they have made peace with it. They trust that God knows what is going on and will make good come from bad. I think that if I can help other people find hope in God, then that is worth losing my arm for.

My friend Sarah says that I get to be the voice of God. I usually roll my eyes when she says it, because if I were God, I would never have chosen me, of all people, to speak for Him! There are a lot of other people who can say things better than I can. But it is His plan and for reasons I don't understand, at least for a while, He has chosen me to say what He wants people to know; that He is real, that He loves them, that they can know Him and trust Him. Maybe he picked me because I tell it like it is: I don't know how to sound smart or sophisticated in interviews. I just say what's in my heart and hopefully my mouth cooperates!

And I am thankful. I could have died. I could have been really mangled. I could have been hurt so bad that I might not have been able to surf again. I have lots and lots of things to be thankful for.

I don't really want people looking to me for inspiration. I just want to be a sign along the way that points toward heaven. I think that God probably did talk to Sarah on the way to the hospital. That verse He brought to her mind was not just for my brother, my mom or for me. I think it's for every person who is feeling down or defeated or a little lost in life, perhaps angry or frustrated by what's going on: "'For I know the plans I have for you,' declares the LORD, 'plans to prosper you and not to harm you, plans to give you hope and a future.'"

I'm proud to be part of God's plans, and I hope, in some small way, this surfer girl from Hawaii can make Him proud, too.

that was then, this is now...

> "I believe God made me for a purpose,
> but he also made me fast, and when I run,
> I feel God's pleasure."
> —OLYMPIC RUNNER ERIC LIDDELL

Has it really been five years since I first wrote *Soul Surfer*? Crazy! All of that excitement surrounding my book, all those interviews and appearances and hearing about it climbing up the bestseller list . . . that feels like *so* long ago. So much has happened since, it's all kind of a big blur. When people ask me, "Bethany, what have you done since then?" I usually shrug and reply, "I don't even know where to begin!" My dog Ginger passed away and I got a new puppy shar-pei, Hana.

My older brother, Noah, got married. I went sky-diving—twice! My family started the Friends of Bethany Foundation to help shark attack survivors and amputees. There have been book signings, appearances, and travels around the world for surf trips, competitions, and mission trips: overall just sharing my story, hopefully inspiring others to live their lives to the fullest.

And of course, I've been surfing. For me, it's like breathing: something that's so a part of me, I can't imagine living without it. My hand and feet are constantly wrinkled and waterlogged, I am in the water so much! I've definitely grown and excelled a lot in my surfing, and that's given me an even stronger love and passion for the sport. From barrel riding to big wave surfing, I've just fallen in love with the *art* of riding waves. Surfing competitions have taken me from one corner of the globe to the other, and I thrill at every victory and agonize over every defeat. I try not to dwell on the losses too long, though! I am very competitive. And I think that's a good thing. I think knowing what you want and going for it is something every-one should strive to do.

I'm the same person I always was, but I also feel like I've grown so much, too. It's like part of me is still the same surf grom who craves the waves while the other part of me is thinking about life and the future. One thing for sure hasn't changed: I am still always following my dream and follow-ing the path that God sets before me. I may have no clue where I'm going, but He sure does! A lot of teens feel this way, I know. You graduate high school and you're like, "What now?" I can relate. It's like all of a sudden, you're face-to-face with your future and its one giant question mark. What will I do? Who will I be?

I think part of growing up is finding your faith. It's faith in God, faith in yourself, faith that everyone has a gift, a talent, and a purpose. God wants you to pursue your gift to the fullest of your ability. That's doing His work. And if you're not quite sure what that gift is, then have faith it will come to you when you're ready to accept it. I am always kind of shell-shocked when something incredible or new comes my way. Sometimes I'm scared, because it's something I have never done or tried before and I'm not sure I'll be a success. Well, it's like the first time you get on a surfboard. Of course you're gonna fall off, then fall off again, and again and again . . . till you get your footing and your balance. The more you try, the more you refuse to give up, the better you get at riding the waves.

So in the course of these past five years, a lot of amazing opportunities have been placed before me. The most incredible is the making of *Soul Surfer* into a major motion picture. Okay, reality check here: *me* as a movie? My friends are having a good laugh at that one. I am *not* the kind of person who wants to be a movie star or even famous. I am just a fairly normal young adult—despite what people have in their minds about me.

Once I got over the initial shock of my life playing on giant screens around the world, I thought, "Well, why not? If this is what God has in mind, if this will take my message, His message, and bring it to an even larger audience, then why not?" So *Soul Surfer* is now a movie starring AnnaSophia Robb, Helen Hunt, Dennis Quaid, Lorraine Nicholson, and Carrie Underwood, in theaters April 15, 2011. Seriously, it has been an amazing experience making this film, from the first meetings with the director to casting, filming the stunts, and seeing it all edited together.

I've kept a movie journal—just for you!—so I could share all the special (and crazy!) moments along the way. When I look back now, I can't believe it's all finished, and I'm going to get to see the final product. It was a journey for sure, for everyone involved. But I think we've all grown for having gone through it together. At least I know I have!

my top 5 favorite moments over the past five years

1. surfing 'round the world (Brazil, Australia, Indonesia, Portugal, South Africa, Puerto Rico, Tahiti)

Not many girls my age can say they've been all over the world—I'm so blessed. My surfing competitions take me to practically every corner of the globe. When there's downtime during the competition waiting period, I try to venture out and explore the area. Like when I went to Europe in 2010, I got to go to Paris, France, with a few friends and just enjoy some art and history in one of the most beautiful cities in the world! I like to try the local healthy (or sometimes not that healthy) food, and occasionally get to hang out with a local family or friends and see what their lifestyle is like.

Here's how it goes when I hit a new locale for a competition: Sometimes I'll have to travel as much as 36 hours to get to the destination. First I have to adjust to the time zone and get my bearings of the area. After settling in, I head for the competition zone and try to surf there no matter what the conditions (which are usually not the best). I need time to adjust to the water temperature, the difference in the waves, and the tide changes (some places have really extreme tides). Then I just rest and try to get my mind set and focused for competition. Once the contest starts, it's all about getting two good wave scores in twenty to thirty minutes. You want to get good or excellent scores, and only your best two count. Though it sounds easy, this can often be really challenging. This is why I train every day—because I want to become the best surfer I can be. And hopefully that will be reflected in my competition results.

In surfing, unlike other sports, there are a lot of different factors. Sometimes the wave conditions factor higher than your surf competitors. Sometimes your competition results don't reflect your talent as a surfer, but sometimes they do.

Right now I am ranked in the top 25 in the world along with my friends Alana Blanchard and Carissa Moore. But I know that I have the ability to excel on any day. My highlight was finishing number two by half a point in the World Junior Pro in Australia in January 2009.

2. getting straight, strong, and healthy

In 2010, I started correcting my posture (spinal alignment) through Dillberg Integrated Healthcare. (Hey, I'm sitting up straight now as I write!) I believe posture has a huge effect on your health. I have really enjoyed learning about it and reading up on this subject. I never would have thought that misalignment could cause everything from bad digestion to headaches. But it does!

For me, it's kind of a different situation because I have one arm. But I feel that it's important for everyone (whether you have four limbs or no limbs) to make posture a priority. I'm working on correcting my posture through several different exercises that were designed specifically for me. Also with Dillberg Integrated Healthcare, I've been working on building my strength to better my surfing and overall fitness. They've put together a customized program that I can take on the road when I travel!

In recent years, I've also realized that diet plays a huge role in your body's health and performance. I began to notice that when I eat well, I have great energy, and when I don't, I just don't feel as energetic. My diet now consists of mostly organic foods, lots of vegetables, fresh fish, sprouted beans, sprouts, fruit, nuts and seeds, and a little dark chocolate here and there!

Even if I weren't a pro surfer, I would still eat this way. It's one of the aspects of health that we can somewhat control. We can't fully control our surroundings and the toxins and chemicals that exist in the places we go, but at least we can do our part to contribute to good health by what we put in our bodies. It's been really amazing to learn about this and then actually see its affect on my life!

3. the children of Thailand

In 2005, It was really exciting for me when World Vision, a Christian relief, development, and advocacy organization dedicated to working with children, families, and communities to overcome poverty and injustice, asked me to go to Thailand. My friend, youth pastor Sarah Hill, encouraged me to go. Thailand had recently been hit by a tsunami, and though it was almost a year later, the people were still in great need and still trying to recover their lives.

When I was there, it was an incredibly powerful experience—truly faith in action. The area had been devastated by the tsunami that took homes and families. People—particularly children—were terrified to get back into the water. I know this feeling; I was scared the first time I got back in the waves after I lost my arm. But I was able to put my faith in God and allow Him to guide me. This is how I helped a little boy get back into the water and a group of other kids, too. We did surf lessons and just had fun together playing in the ocean. I think it encouraged the parents, too, watching the kids surf and have fun in the ocean. Once they could heal, their future as fishermen was preserved. I visited a few people's homes and an orphanage, and became friends with a young girl, Ketsara, who had lost her mom and brother in the tsunami. She, like me, realized that oftentimes good things come out of our bad experiences. Another thing that was really cool was that World Vision was helping the people build their traditional Thai fishing boats so they could get back out there and provide for their families.

4. Make a Wish Foundation

Two young girls, Lauren and Katherine, wanted me to teach them surfing. They both had chronic illnesses. Lauren had chronic adhesive arachnoiditis, and Katie had cystic fibrosis. They had both requested as their "wish" to meet me. So the Make a Wish Foundation flew them and their families out to Hawaii so we could spend some time together. I was so honored to meet such inspiring souls. I can't even describe how amazing it made me feel to put a smile on their faces. We did a surf lesson with the girls at Hanalei Bay, near the pier, where I learned to surf when I was little. It's so gnarly to have such a bad illness at such a young age—it breaks my heart. The girls are just normal, fun-loving kids and it feels so wrong that they have to deal with all that. In our time together, we just mainly focused on having fun and enjoying life, and that's what I encouraged them to do! Every day is a blessing.

5. Mexico

Almost every year my church youth group goes on a mission trip to Tijuana, Mexico. We meet up with Spectrum Ministries in San Diego, then head across the border. Our goals as a group are to go in and help the orphanages with whatever they need help with. It could be anything from feeding, bathing, and playing with kids to building or painting. Just anything! Whatever they ask us to do. Most important, our priority is to just love the kids and be a light, sharing Jesus's love.

One day of the trip, we go into town and set up showers and stations where kids can get clean, get their hair brushed, and get new clothes and shoes. My task on one of the bathhouse days was washing the kids' feet. Washing their feet was really cool because that's what Jesus did for the disciples. It symbolizes being cleansed of your sins. It was hard to know whether any of them knew Jesus 'cause I don't speak Spanish, and they don't speak English. But it was really cool to do something so simple for them since they have so little. The kids were adorable and they just liked having attention from all of us older kids!

We also go to the dump—where families actually live—and pass out food. It's really sad to see the living conditions for the people there. It was just crazy handing food to them and seeing how grateful they were. They live their lives scrounging for scraps, or trying to find stuff in the junkyard that they can sell to buy some food. It was humbling to see how grateful and excited they were. The whole experience just encourages me to know how blessed I am not having to worry about what and when I'm going to eat next. And just to be thankful for everything I have! Overall, it's just really fun hanging out with the little kids and stepping into a whole different world.

my movie journal

The experience of making a movie of *Soul Surfer* was one I will never forget. I wanted to share it with all of you to give you a peek into what it's like behind the scenes on a set. There were lots of things I never expected, and a lot of "movie magic" that just blew me away. I like to think of this process as a journey in which I made lots of incredible new friends and family (like AnnaSophia Robb and director Sean McNamara), and once again I learned to put my faith in God and trust He would lead me on the right path. I think we all felt His presence while making this film. . . .

December 1, 2009

So I just found out that Sony Pictures is going to distribute *Soul Surfer*. We have been talking to producers and Hollywood executives for a long, loooong time—really ever since we released the original book and it got so much great attention. That was about five years ago! We've been through several scripts, several production companies, and lots of setbacks. But I'll admit: I never thought it would really happen. I was kind of like, "Yeah, sure . . ." But then the wheels started to turn. We got a director. Then a financier. Then a script that everyone liked. And now we have a signed and sealed distribution deal with one of the biggest movie companies in Hollywood. Wow. That's pretty much all I can say at this moment. I'm a little in shock, because the thought of me and my family's life up on a huge movie screen . . . well, it's weird. And quite nerve-racking. But at the same time, I am beyond stoked, because I know that this is going to take my message to a whole new level.

If I can reach out to millions of moviegoers and help them find faith and God . . . well, it's a huge gift for me. What I really want is to create an impactful movie that changes lives. And as always, God steps in and shows me the way. He always has plans for me. I just have to ride the wave, wherever He takes me . . . and trust that my family won't come off looking cheesy on the big screen!

December 10, 2009

I just got an e-mail saying that AnnaSophia Robb has been cast to play me in the movie. I'm really happy, and really stoked. She's a great actress! My mom and I had actually seen her in *Bridge to Terabithia*, and we suggested she play me. She also starred in *Charlie and the Chocolate Factory, Samantha: An American Girl Movie, Return to Witch Mountain, Because of Winn Dixie*, and others. She says on her website that she's really committed to a lot of charity organizations and believes in changing the world for the better. My kind of girl! I think she'll totally get me, and she'll really be able to understand how and why I do what I do. One thing I really like about Anna-Sophia is her *eyes*. She really just brings the passion, drama, and emotions that she needs to show in a scene through her eyes. It's beautiful, and it really shows how important and serious a role is to her. They say the eyes reflect the soul. I can't believe she's only 16; she's so mature and accomplished for that age! I'm so blessed to have her starring as me. The only thing that kind of makes me laugh—she's really small! I'm like 5'11", and she's maybe 5'2"? Well, hopefully movie magic will make her look more my size! And of course, I'm also a little concerned because they tell me she's never been on a surfboard before. But I plan on fixing that real soon!

December 14, 2009

Big night tonight! We went out to dinner at a restaurant in Hanalei with my family, my manager [at the time], Roy, and the VPs from Sony Pictures' Affirm Films, Rich Peluso and Steve Okin. Well, actually, first I was surfing, and I came in from the waves and saw them on the beach, watching me. That's where we initially met, which seems just right, since the waves are my home and where much of the movie is gonna take place. My first thoughts: They are really nice guys. Not all Hollywood slick as I imagined they might be! I am really blessed to have them on board. In a lot of ways they understand me 'cause they believe in Jesus as well. It's a relief to know that we share that as a team. They're from Tennessee, and they both have a lot of kids, so they're used to dealing with lots of energy and chaos! We told them that this movie's gotta be done right, 'cause we're gonna live with it for the rest of our lives. And *hello*? This is *my life* we're showing to everybody who sees the movie. It has to be real; it has to look like and sound like me and my family and friends. I am all about the truth; you will never hear me embellish something or lie, because I know that God wants me to tell my truth and His truth. So yeah, I'm sure it's really tempting to get all special FX and dramatic with stuff—it's a movie, and that's what movies do. There's, like, music playing in the background while I surf (that never happens in real life, trust me!). But I also don't want them to lose sight of what's really important to me—the reason we're doing this. Rich and Steve nodded; they understand how it's way more to me than a movie. But dinner was great, and my family all got to meet them. It was pretty low-key, we just got to chat and get to know each other. I'm feeling real good about how things are going so far!

December 15, 2009

Tonight we had a BBQ with a bunch of the movie crew. I couldn't even begin to name all the people who were there! There were probably about ten guys, all here for some part of the movie. It feels like all the pieces of this puzzle are beginning to come together! I got to chat with the main producers, and also the director, Sean McNamara, and he showed me some really cool stuff on his computer. He showed us how he'll make AnnaSophia look like she has one arm. It's really cool how they do it—kind of like the effect in *Forrest Gump* when the actor has to play a soldier who has lost his legs. She wears a green sleeve on her left arm (kind of like a green screen), and above it she wears a prosthetic that looks like my stump. With some special digital effects, the arm "disappears" and the stump remains. It looks *exactly* like what my arm looks like. I can't wait to see how it looks in action in the movie.

They also showed us drawings of the screenplay, the storyboard. The artist was really good at capturing the action! It seemed like it would take a long time to create this—each little picture was drawn with great detail. And they were really pretty! Not just sketches or scribbles, but works of art. I remember when I was little, I did "Video Morning News Crew" at Hanalei Elementary School, and our teacher, Ms. Hermstad, made us draw play-by-play storyboards for our "broadcast." Mine didn't look nearly as good as these, but I remember the process. It helps you map out the sequence of action and what the camera will be capturing—every angle and what the viewer will be seeing.

Everyone was really nice. It was great meeting all those guys and just having them come out to meet our family on Kauai, and seeing where we live. They did a lot of location scouting all over the island, trying to get an idea of the different locations where scenes in the movie took place in real life. They also watched me surf—which made me a little bit nervous 'cause then I was under pressure to perform. I didn't want to disappoint! The best part of the day: They got to see our glorious sunset on the beach. What I like to think of as God painting his storyboard on the sky!

December 18, 2009

So I talked to AnnaSophia for the first time yesterday. I wasn't really nervous for the call—I'm just not that kind of person to get nervous about those types of things. But then, when I was talking to her, I did notice I was stuttering a little, and I couldn't think of what to say. Lot of looooong pauses! Okay—maybe I was a little uneasy. I didn't know if we had anything in common. But she was so sweet and I really liked her instantly; I think she felt the same way. We just clicked. I think she's gonna be a great girl for the role. She is really motivated to work hard, and she told me she's getting ready to start training physically. She told me she's gonna start swimming a lot and working with a trainer who will hopefully teach her a lot of balance work, so she'll be able to balance on the surfboard. She'll also work on leg and arm strengthening, so she'll be able to get up with one or two arms. It's not easy, and I know she has a long road ahead of her.

She said she couldn't wait to come out here and meet me and my family, to learn more about her role, who I am, and who our family is as a whole. I can't wait to meet her in person and get to know her more. I told her she should come out to Hawaii sooner rather than later 'cause I'm leaving for a surf contest in early January. Hopefully, she'll make it out here in late December so we can catch up for a week before I leave. I think it's really important we have one-on-one time, because once the movie starts, she's gonna be so busy, we won't really be able to hang out much. So it'd be great to get to know each other before it all goes down.

AnnaSophia told me she was on her way to a sleepover with all her cousins! It's like an annual thing they do. We also talked about her school. She's in tenth grade, and she goes to public school in Colorado. She said it's a pretty small community-type town/area, the same as Hawaii or Kauai, so that was cool. We have something in common! She told me she's never surfed, but she snowboards and she's pretty good at swimming. I think she'll be really confident in the water. I can't wait to show her how I live and get her out there surfing!

January 2, 2010

AnnaSophia came out to Kauai to learn to surf and meet my family and me. The first time we met was a little awkward. Honestly, I was at first a little shocked: She's really cute, but she's also really tiny! Plus she has no tan! It's hard for me to picture her playing me! But you can't judge a book by its cover, right? She might look small and sweet, but I do think she has a lot of inner strength. She came with her youth leader and friend, Rachel. It was just really fun having them out. I took her to learn how to surf where I learned to surf, in Hanalei. And her very first time, she did *really* well. She was *ripping*! Getting waves! Standing up fast! She only ate it, like, twice. It was sick!

After surfing, I took her on a hike to my favorite beach. She and Rachel just cruised on the beach with my dog, Hana, while I surfed. Hana was just rambling all over the beach. And she met a lot of people 'cause everyone knew who Hana was. So she got to meet a lot of our friends. Then we made dinner together, and just chatted about anything and everything. It was really fun. I think she's just great, and I adore her!

January 3, 2010

AnnaSophia got to come to church with us at Calvary Chapel North Shore in Kilauea. It was really fun. She's a Christian as well, so it's cool that we can share that in common. Beyond all the movie stuff and whatever is going on, we can still just talk to each other about what we believe. And it makes us better friends. And I'm just so glad that she can be a good light and shine in the industry that she's working in.

After church, I introduced her to Sarah Hill, who's one of my best friends. And she was always there for me since I was a younger girl, just to talk to and encourage me. It was kind of funny 'cause AnnaSophia brought out her friend Rachel, who's kind of like a Sarah to AnnaSophia. And it was just fun for us all to get together and eat lunch and talk and share everything that we have in common, and everything that we don't have in common! We talked about food, boys, activities, our faith, our families, books, and whatever popped in our minds!

January 4, 2010

AnnaSophia took some surfing lessons today from my coach, Russell Lewis, who is an *amazing* coach. He grew up in Australia, and he was one of the best surfers there in the prime of his youth. He's been coaching me since I was eight or nine. Russell has this gift: he knows how to teach everyone from pros to complete beginners. He did a great job with AnnaSophia; he taught her about the ocean, how it works and how to be safe out there and feel comfortable. Then he got into some of the techniques, and by the second day she was already catching waves on her own and kind of turning, which is *really* hard for a beginner. Surfing is one of those sports that's not easy to learn—it looks a lot easier than it is. But I think AnnaSophia is a natural! I'm proud of her!

There was one pretty funny moment, though—funny for me, scary for her! While she and Russell were practicing, the lifeguards started yelling at this guy to come in from the ocean. Turns out the guy was just doing something reckless and the guards called him out, but AnnaSophia and Russell didn't hear what the lifeguard said. They thought it was a shark sighting and freaked out! They paddled in as fast as they could to the beach— where I was laughing. We all ended up having a good laugh about it. Then she went back out to catch a few more.

January 17–18, 2010

My family and I flew to Oahu for a script reading. We've been waiting an eternity to see this script, and now it's two weeks before production and we're just getting a look? *Are you kidding me!* It's been frustrating to say the least. We were all super nervous, wondering, "Is this script gonna be good? Is it gonna be real—or really Hollywood?" We met up with all the producers, directors, and writers and spent the full day listening to them read the script. We highlighted everything we didn't like, and put a star by the things we did like. I have to say I sure highlighted a lot of stuff! Things that just didn't sound like me, or seemed a little hokey. There was some really kooky, funny stuff. But overall we were all pretty happy with it. We went over it again and again, editing, suggesting, changing lines and scenes! Everyone was really receptive to our ideas and I felt like it was really a team effort. I was surprised how draining the day was, but mentally, you gotta stay focused. So much for glamour . . . this is what making a movie is really all about. Collaborating to make it the best picture it can be.

January 25, 2010

AnnaSophia and I were walking up to the head office at Turtle Bay today. We bumped into this older guy, and AnnaSophia started chatting with him. He said, "Hi, Bethany," but he didn't tell me his name. Obviously he knew who I was (hmmm . . . did the one arm give me away?)! And though he looked familiar, I couldn't put my finger on who he was. Well, he ended up being my "dad" in the movie, Dennis Quaid! And it was just kind of funny 'cause I didn't recognize him. But he's super gracious and easy to talk to. We both got a laugh over it. I am just so Hawaii, not Hollywood! I don't spend my time obsessing over famous people!

I have to admit, today was the first day all this movie stuff felt "real." I saw all the offices and the wardrobe room set up, and many of the actors arriving and prepping, there's a ton of script rewrites being made based on our suggestions. All kinds of stuff going on! That's when it really hit me and reality sunk in: "Whoa, there's a movie being made about me and my family."

January 28, 2010

Tonight we had Helen Hunt over for dinner. Helen is also a really well-known actress—she's starred in a ton of movies and TV shows and now she's playing my "mom" in the movie. She was super cool, easy to talk to, and I think she's gonna be great as my mom. AnnaSophia came over too, and they got along really well—which I think is important so they can work well together. I was really hoping they'd click, because my mom and I are super close, and our relationship is so special and a key source of strength in my life. I made some pesto for the dinner (my specialty!), and they were lovin' it! It was just nice for my mom to get to know Helen and share some stories, so Helen can get into the heart of her character. My mom is amazing; she has a unique outlook on life and is always encouraging me to be the best I can be at whatever I do. Another cool thing I found out was that Helen surfs! Kind of a surprise to me! I guess she's been surfing for a few years now.

I haven't surfed with her yet, but I look forward to it!

February 1, 2010

So as I said before, my initial feelings about making the movie: stunned. Just like, "Really, a movie about me?" It seemed such a stretch—like this distant possibility. But now that it's real, it's actually happening, I'm starting to worry a little. Part of me is thinking, "Okay, my life's probably gonna go crazy (or crazier) after the movie." So "privacy" won't really be a word in my life anymore. Which is kind of stressful, but I'm gonna have to deal with it. Again, I have to trust that God has a plan here; He knows what He's doing. He knows what I can do. I see this movie as a good thing, a great thing for sure. But I guess all great things also come with some sacrifice? Maybe I won't be able to just walk down a street anymore without being recognized. I asked AnnaSophia if that happens to her, and she said, "Sometimes." But it's part of her job, part of the price you pay. And I have to keep reminding myself *why* we're doing this movie. Not to become famous, but to spread God's message and my story. To inspire people to never give up faith.

February 2, 2010

It's the opening day of shooting the movie! We're on Oahu, where they're going to be filming everything. We asked my really good friend Pastor Mike Stangel to come down and pray for the movie and start it off right. Just having everyone—there was like more than 100 people there—gather in prayer was incredibly powerful. It was a really special day. I had a few of my friends visiting, hanging out with me, checking out the set. I felt like I had a lot of support!

The first scene they shot was in the local grocery store. AnnaSophia (as me!) goes in shopping with one arm. She struggles a lot, and as she drops groceries, people stare at her. The scene felt very real for me, like a slice out of my own life, because

I've had moments in the grocery store where I get really frustrated, especially in the produce section when I'm trying to rip the bag off, open it, then put the apples in. I watched AnnaSophia do the same thing, and I could see the frustration in her face—and also the embarrassment as people watch her, pity her, whisper behind her back. It felt so real for me and it's something I deal with all the time. People can't help but stare I guess—with one arm, really blond hair, and given how tall I am, I guess I kind of stand out! But I get really frustrated and it gets annoying. I told this to Sean, our director, and he used a lot of my suggestions and emotions in the scene. I watched AnnaSophia in character drop the apples on the ground; I can see there are tears just about to well in her eyes, but she holds them back. She's stronger than that; so am I.

February 3, 2010

The second day of shooting: Alana and Bethany go shopping and they bump into Malina—a fictional surf competitor—and kind of have a little catfight. In reality, I'm pretty good friends with all my competitors and stuff like that doesn't really happen, but I guess it adds more drama to the story. So, yeah . . . I kind of hope some of that scene gets edited out in postproduction! I hate to come off catty!

I went over to the video village, where they have a bunch of director's chairs set up for the producers, actors, and of course the director. You can sit there and watch the scene being filmed on little TVs. Well, guess what? They made a chair with my name on it! That was pretty exciting and cool for me.

February 3, 2010

One scene in the movie that I was really skeptical about was the Alana photo shoot scene—and that's what we were shooting today. I just wanted to make sure that the character Alana is modest and it isn't a risqué scene. I mean, I want her to be a good role model. I want to encourage girls to like themselves as they are and not feel like they have to be a certain way—like super skinny. The photo shoot scene is a made-up scene for the story. In the story Bethany and Alana are supposed to do the shoot together, but since Bethany lost her arm, she can't do it. But Bethany knows Alana wants to do it, so she encourages her to do it anyway. My main concern was that Alana's character isn't wearing a really skimpy bikini. I mean in the surfing world, people wear bikinis, I do too, and that's just how it is. But I was encouraging the filmmakers to choose a more modest one. And they did. The scene is still not my favorite. I just hope that it doesn't send the wrong message.

February 9, 2010

Today we shot the Thailand scene. They set up near an old, run-down building and property the whole area of "Thailand"; they had live animals cruising around, and Thai people. You would never know you were in Hawaii. I actually got to have a cameo! I was one of the other missionary kids in the youth group. So, watch out for me when you see the movie . . . I'll be riding in the bus and carrying a box of soccer balls. It was pretty fun, but I actually had to wait all day long, so I was really over it. It was hot and sweaty out that day. But I'm glad I did it, and it should be funny to see myself alongside Carrie Underwood and AnnaSophia. The Thailand scene, I think, is one of the coolest scenes in the movie—it's just so different from the rest of the movie.

February 13, 2010

They shot the church scene today, and I went down to watch to see if there were any tips I could throw out there. At first, I was kind of frustrated when I first started watching the scene. For me going to church is exciting; I'm happy to go and I enjoy it! But all the extras and actors in the scene looked so somber and bored—like they were at a funeral! So

I got up out of my seat and went over and re-minded everyone that this is church—and we're praising the God of all creation who loves us! I explained that church is a place to express my joy for God and my family's joy for God. They got it. In the next take, their faces were more lit up and they actually looked like they were happy to be there. Now that's what church is about! Glad I could help out . . .

February 25, 2010

When it came to shooting the hospital scene, my mom and grandma came to watch with me. I think they were worried how it might make me feel. But honestly, for me it isn't emotional to watch it being filmed. I can't really explain why though. Maybe 'cause there are the cameras and the crew and all these people standing around, running around doing their jobs. It's not like sitting in the theater, or real life at all. I felt kind of distant from it . . . and I was glad for that.

February 26, 2010

Throughout the filming of the movie there was this side group documenting the movie called the EPK (Electronic Press Kit) crew. I did a couple of interviews with them and I also got to "host" my own behind-the-scenes tour. That was pretty fun. Today, I went down when they were shooting the Turtle Bay contest. I got to interview a bunch of my friends who were doing stunt surfing in the water. That was fun 'cause they are like my real friends and interviewing them was kind of funny. I giggled when I was asking questions—me being serious around my friends is a tough thing! But hopefully it turns out okay!

March 4, 2010

When I show up on set, pretty much the first place I go to is the specialty truck with all the snacks. Then I head to the second snack tent and get a green tea. I'm pretty at home on the set now! I just roam around, saying hi to everyone. It's fun 'cause it's like one big family. Everyone's just cruising around, doing what they gotta do. Both my brothers, Noah and Tim, are working on the set, and my sister-in-law Becky, too. Tim is a production assistant (PA) in the camera department. And Noah and Becky are coproducers.

When a movie is being made about you, you obviously want your friends, family, and community to be receptive and supportive of the project. For my family, it was very important, especially considering that we live on a small island, and the surfing community is small. It was critical for us to have our real-life community as excited about the movie as possible. Plus, it helps make the story more true to life, and for me it's a tribute to them for being a part of my life and story. And for most of us, it's cool to see how a movie is made, so I'm glad to be able to share that experience together.

While filming the movie, my family and I had a lot of good friends who would come and be extras for the day. Some of my best friends flew over to be extras. Extras are the people in the scene who don't have any speaking lines. Having good family friends working on the movie, being extras in the movie, stunt surfers, etc., made the process really special for us. It was fun to see them all take part in it. We even had a really good friend, Sonya Balmores-Chung, star as the fictional character Malina in the movie. It was really cool to see Sonya in action!

March 7, 2010

I shot some more of the EPK today. Sean (the director) and I got to host a tour of the house set. I just adore Sean and love being around him. He's easy to talk with and a fun guy to be around! So it was fun, he and I just walking around, showing where Dennis drives over the bush; showing "my dad's" work shed, where he makes up the handle for my board; my bedroom, my kitchen. The set is at a house being rented as the Hamilton family house. It's not our real-life home (phew!) because my mom would *freak*.

March 9, 2010

I had to leave three weeks before they finished filming, which was kind of a bummer. Leaving the movie and all the actors and crew I had become friends with was a little bittersweet. We had all become good friends and just had a special bond as they are now a major part of my life. But I just really want to continue my goals in surfing . . . so back to business and bye-bye Hollywood for now!

March 10, 2010

I am headed to Australia, and today Hana *finally* made her debut as an actor in the movie! Hana's my dog and she's playing the role as my late dog, Ginger, so I was kind of sad that I missed that. But I got to see a video of her. And she's so cute! I don't know if she's got that full natural talent, but she's beautiful and I'm so glad that she got to be in the movie.

March 19, 2010

Today is the last day of filming. Though thousands of miles and an ocean away, I am just thinking about it and I really hope that they got everything they need. The movie now goes into the editing process back in Los Angeles, California. Though the filming is done, there's still a huge part of the filmmaking left. This is where the story really comes together. Scenes may change, reorganize, or even be removed. Music is added, sound effects, visual effects, and lots of other things I don't even know about!

April 21, 2010

Becky and I are on our way to Europe for a few surf competitions. We stopped over in California to visit the editing room and see the progress that is being made on *Soul Surfer*. They just have a few scenes cut together at this point. Sean, the director, met up with us and showed us a few scenes—which was really cool to see—and we had lunch on the Sony lot with a few of the executives overseeing the project. I wanted to make it very clear to them how important the movie is to me and my family— especially that the surfing is realistic and really impressive, and that my faith in God is apparent. Also, that the Hawaiian culture and lifestyle is captured and respected. They seemed to hear my points, but we'll see!

June 19, 2010

I took a break from my surf trip in Tahiti and flew to California to watch an early cut of *Soul Surfer*. I was really nervous to see it. I wasn't sure that the movie could be all that I'd hoped it could be. So I said a little prayer . . .

My mom and I met up with Sean and sat down in a private theater to watch it. As I watched it, I experienced many different emotions. I laughed, I cried, I got annoyed; I felt defeat, frustration, determination, victory.

I loved the relationship that my dad and I share throughout the film! I loved seeing my dog Hana star as my late dog Ginger—she's adorable! Also Dennis and Helen did some of their own stunt surfing in the movie and they were quite impressive! AnnaSophia was definitely the star of the film. She did great, and I am so grateful to have her play me.

The emotions I felt on a more personal level were different. It's hard to truly share them all. I guess I have some pretty huge expectations! I want this movie to show the power and love that Jesus had and has for me—that same power and love that He has for anyone. The movie has a great story and is very entertaining, but above all I want it to inspire people. I told Sean how I feel, and he gets it. It's just the first cut, and there's more work to do.

The surfing was also discouraging for me. Surfing is the essence of my life. So it's obviously really important to have good surfing in the movie. From the first cut, I could tell the surfing needs work. There is not much surfing done by me. I'm hoping to improve that by going to Tahiti with the movie crew next month! I know as the *Soul Surfer* team continues to work every day, it will only get better! It's exciting to see the process of a movie being made. So many details, tons of planning, and a great deal of patience and perseverance. It's one mega family!

I'm ever so grateful to my family and of course to the *Soul Surfer* team for all their hard work! Most of all grateful to Jesus Christ! Proverbs 3:5–6, "Trust in the LORD with all your heart, and lean not on your own understanding; In all your ways acknowledge Him, and He shall direct your paths."

July 26, 2010

I'm in Tahiti right now with the director and a few surf cinematographers. We came down with a small crew for five days, hoping to get some really good beautiful surf. We got a little nervous in the beginning because the forecast looked a little sketchy. Plus there were passing squalls. But every

day the conditions have cleaned up and we've gotten really good surf! Thank God! Our family had
been praying and hoping for this. I hope you enjoy
the surfing in the movie!

October 12, 2010

On my way home from a surf competition in Portugal, I got a call from Sean that I needed to come
over to California immediately to view the final
cut of the picture before it gets "locked." So we
changed my flights, and stopped over before going
home. My dad, my brother Noah, and my manager Thayer all watched the movie, and submitted
a few notes and concerns we have. Overall we all
really liked how it came together and think it's
going to be a very moving film. The producers/
filmmakers seem to be open to making a few
changes based on our notes. It's really awesome
that they are allowing us to be involved and share
our opinions. We obviously want to be able to take
pride in the movie, and they recognize that.

The main phases left now in the making of the movie are the sound (music, sound effects, and mixing), the visual effects, and the color correction. Music is really important to me. I want the movie to be filled with positive music with a good message—no bad lyrics or immoral themes. Hopefully my family will get to help them with that. Then I think the final product gets put back onto film, and reproduced and sent to your local theater! It still has several months to go, but I'm really looking forward to seeing the final product!

even a surfer can survive Hollywood!

So now, I can truly say, "There's a movie made about my life." It's been quite a ride, filled with ups and downs, pumps and stalls, maybe even a few wipeouts. But in the end, it's something I am incredibly proud of. One thing I was really impressed with—and grateful for—was how passionate and motivated the whole team was to make a good story and movie. They may not have always agreed or shared the same feelings or faith, but they allowed my family to tell our story in a way that was truthful and inspiring. It was a really fun experience, but often stressful as well, so I'm quite honestly glad that it's wrapped (that's movie talk for "finished"!). It's such an amazing movie to see. I really hope audiences watch it not only with their eyes but with their hearts. I thank God for the opportunity and for getting my family through it. I can't wait to see what impact *Soul Surfer* has on moviegoers who may not have read my book or heard of me. I'm excited to see people discover their faith, and I'm excited to spread God's message in such a big, bold, beautiful way!

final thoughts ...

the most frustrating thing about making a movie

One thing that honestly was a bit annoying for me—'cause I don't have much patience—is that they seriously spend a half a day or more on just one scene! I was like, "Come on! Let's just get this over with!" I got bored a lot; I usually couldn't last more than two hours on the set!

the most surprising thing about making a movie

One of the craziest things that I learned about shooting a movie is that it's shot totally out of order. Like in *Soul Surfer,* the first scene we shot was a one-arm scene with AnnaSophia. So obviously it's like way out of order—if we were actually following the way things happened, she wouldn't have lost her arm yet! Then right after that, they shot a scene that happens earlier in the movie. So that was kind of weird. But then when you see the movie all come together, it's seamless. That's the magic of moviemaking, I guess!

shooting a surfing scene—pressure's on

Shooting the surfing scenes for the movie is quite challenging, mainly due to the fact that you have to kind of be "on hold" for the ocean. Sometimes, the weather and waves just refuse to cooperate! We did a lot of standing around, hoping the waves would get good for shooting. But once the waves were good, we had a good crew, so we girls just had to surf! Which was fun, but then the pressure is on.

inside scoop on the actors

Honestly. I guess everyone who starred as my family is kind of how I expected them to be. Our family is really laid-back. My brothers and I were born and raised in Kauai, so we're more kind of on cruise control. The actors are definitely different than us. But they all did a really good job acting— doing their job, becoming something they're not. So I was really blessed to have each and every one of those actors portray our family.

Dennis Quaid as my dad . . . I think he's perfect for the part. He's really into golf, so he and my dad went golfing a few times throughout the film. Thanks to *Soul Surfer* he got bitten by the surfing bug! He's pretty much out there every day! He even goes on his own now. I surfed with him a few times, and he's a natural. He's got that little surfer touch.

He's pretty funny, and quite the entertainer. At the occasional crew get-together he would play a song on the piano or guitar. One important thing is that he really wants what our family wanted for the film. So he's really helpful in just figuring out what was true to the story, and how my dad truly is.

Having Helen Hunt be a part of the movie was such a blessing. She's such a great person and so talented. Getting to know her throughout the filming of the movie was really fun. She's a surfer. We got to go surfing together a few times. And she took my mom surfing—my mom hasn't surfed in years, so that was such a breakthrough! It just put the spark right back in my mom's eyes. It was something I haven't seen in a while. I am so thankful to Helen for getting my mom back in the water! Helen's an incredible actress. She's quiet, real down-to-earth. We have a lot of similarities: for example, we like to live healthy. So it's been cool getting to know her. She's kind of just the loving, comforting one in the movie. And she really just brought that motherly touch.

Lorraine Nicholson is playing my good friend Alana Blanchard. Alana and Lorraine—seeing them hang out was pretty hilarious. They look a lot alike, especially after Lorraine gets ready to actually play her role. They're both pretty cruise and mellow. Lorraine and AnnaSophia also really connected, so they were able to portray that deep friendship that Alana and I have. Lorraine is really funny, and she has a hilarious, dramatic perspective on life. One day during filming there was a tsunami threat for Hawaii that was generated from an earthquake in Chile. Shooting the movie was cancelled for that day and everyone fled to high ground. Lorraine has the funniest story from her experience that day! And she'll have you rolling on the floor while she's telling it.

And finally, there's AnnaSophia. I really trusted her to be true to who I am, and she didn't disappoint. We're good friends now, and I feel really blessed to have her in my life.

AnnaSophia Robb

Just the facts!

Birthdate: December 8, 1993

Hails from: Denver, Colorado

Starting out: AnnaSophia began her career on a local church stage at age five in front of 500 people. She studied acting at age eight, and at age nine she and her mom drove to L.A., where after more than forty auditions, she landed a Bratz doll commercial!

Her big roles: In 2005, AnnaSophia was cast in the lead role of Opal opposite Jeff Daniels in *Because of Winn-Dixie*. She's also starred in *An American Girl Holiday, Charlie and the Chocolate Factory, Bridge to Terabithia,* and 2009's *Race to Witch Mountain.*

Upcoming projects: She is currently working on Disney's *Tinker Bell and the Mysterious Winter Woods.* She is the voice of Periwinkle, the winter fairy. AnnaSophia costars with Mae Whitman, Kristin Chenoweth, Raven-Symone, Lucy Liu, and America Ferrera. She also recently completed filming *The Space Between* with director Travis Fine, costarring Melissa Leo.

playing Bethany: an interview with AnnaSophia Robb

before this movie, had you ever surfed?

No! I didn't know how to surf at all, which is pretty funny considering I am playing Bethany Hamilton, one of the greatest surfers of all time, right? I went out to Zuma Beach in California and tried with my dad to surf. It was really fun and two weeks before I went to Hawaii, I was doing four hours a day of training, trying to get my muscles ready for paddling. I had my work cut out for me.

did Bethany teach you a thing or two?

We had three weeks of prep where I would just surf everyday and Bethany would always come out with me, show me how to get up on the board, wait for the right wave . . . . I love it now. But for her, well, it's part of her. She doesn't have to think out there on the waves. I on the other hand . . .

did you and Bethany bond?

When we talked we became close, really good
friends. It was a role that I wanted to play from the
time I heard about it, so I idealized who I thought
she was. I mean, what she went through, how she
survived, her incredible strength, courage, belief in
God . . . . Then I got to know her as a person and
as a friend. I wanted to be as truthful to what she
would have thought. I felt like I was the bridge
between Hollywood and what she wanted. We
would talk a lot, and if I ever had a question I tried
to get her mentality down, so I could make the
emotion as true to her as possible. I felt like it was
an incredible honor to play her, and I knew she put
her trust in me to do it right.

what do you think of Bethany's faith?

Bethany and I are both Christians so that gives us
a lot of common ground and belief. Faith is what
Bethany is really about—trusting in the Lord and

having that faith and that serenity that comes with her. Bethany's just chill. She never gets worked up. She knows someone has her back and there is a bigger picture. I'm kind of in awe. . . .

how is she as an athlete?

She's a serious athlete! She has this mentality that I have never experienced before. She doesn't ever think, "I'm going to go out and risk my life!" She doesn't think about it like that because she loves it so much—but it's a hard-core competitive mentality. When she's in that competition mode and when she sees a wave, she doesn't ever go halfhearted. I focused on that determination when I was playing her. It's really primal and also spiritual.

do you think this role changed you?

Every role I do I feel like it changes me in some way. But just to be able to have a relationship with Bethany, and just seeing her faith shine through in everything she's done, it helps soothe me and help me not worry about the next job. That's something I will now carry with me always.

what was it like getting to know the Hamilton family?

They all wanted to be there, supporting us the whole way through. Helen and Cheri went out surfing a bunch of times. I have never been on a film where it's so connected with a real family. They'd come on set and we'd all be so excited! It gave it so much more meaning. I'd like to think I'm an honorary member of the family now!

Sean McNamara

Just the facts!

Birthdate: May 9, 1962

Nickname: Big Mac

Hails from: Burbank, California

Career highlights: Writer, director, producer. He has worked on numerous feature films and TV shows (including *Raise Your Voice, Race to Space, Even Stevens, That's So Raven, Beyond the Break*) and with stars including Jessica Alba, Shia LaBeouf, Christy Carlson Romano, Hillary Duff, and Raven.

Family man: Three beautiful boys; Mark, Dylan, and Seamus

Proud moment: Ran the L.A. Marathon and finished!

Q&A with director Sean McNamara

how did you decide on AnnaSophia to play Bethany?

When I first asked Bethany whom she wanted to play her, she said AnnaSophia Robb. She told me, "Go rent *Bridge to Terabithia*." So I did, and when I saw her on screen, I knew she was 100 percent right.

how did you come to direct Soul Surfer?

Our casting director came to me with the book. I'm a surfer, so I knew about Bethany and what had been reported in the media. The book sat on my shelf for a while. Then when I read it, I saw there was incredible potential for a movie. But I also I felt like there was something missing, namely the feeling that Bethany had struggled greatly with what had happened. It was really just brushing the surface of the emotions I knew were there. I knew that a movie would need to dig deeper. Unless you see her struggling and overcoming adversity, you don't understand or connect with her. So we met with her agent at the time, Roy Hofstetter—and he sold me. I told him we needed a script. They had one, but it wasn't ready to be a movie. What drew it to me was simply her story and her passion.

so how did you begin working on the new script?

I went and interviewed the Hamilton family for starters. I spent weeks interviewing each of them separately. I used the book for the facts as a guide. But it was the people, the conversations, that gave it more meaning. Talking to Bethany, I could get the crux of what she was feeling. And I also think she's older now, has had more time to cope with it. She realizes more now than she did when she was going through it. And it makes for a really powerful story.

did you have to fictionalize some of what happened to Bethany to make the movie more dramatic?

I tried to stay very true to her story, but yes, we had to put some elements together. For example, we had a little Hawaiian girl who sees Bethany and points and says to her mom, "What happened to her arm?" That didn't happen, but similar things did. So I put all those things together into the mouth of the little girl.

what was your first meeting with Bethany like? what were your first impressions of her?

I met her in church! The service had already started, and she had gotten there late and sat next to me. She gave me a hug, then we listened to a Christian minister go on for an hour! She seemed very shy, very nice. But it also struck me that she was no pushover. She made it pretty clear, "This is how my movie is going to be done," and I respected that.

It was pretty immediate: I really liked her and she liked me. She would sit very close to me when I interviewed people, and I sensed a nervousness of Hollywood, of getting it wrong. She was assertive about two things that were very important to her in making this film: It was all about Jesus, and we had to get the surfing right!

so how did you work together?

I assured Bethany I wasn't interested in making a surfing film. I was interested in making an inspirational movie with surfing as a backdrop. She stayed on the forefront making sure that her Christian ideals made it into the movie and that the surfing was exacting. On this, she was a taskmaster! She even made us go to Tahiti in August to make the surfing look perfect and authentic with bigger, more powerful waves. She was right . . . they look so much better now.

what was the hardest scene to shoot?

I think there were two levels of hard: technical difficult, and when I brought AnnaSophia to the set with her arm "severed" for the first time. I had to walk Bethany and her family on the beach and show them what it was going to look like. The stump was there and the rest of AnnaSophia's arm was in a green sock, which we would digitally remove during editing. It was tense. Bethany's first reaction was to giggle, and then her dad saw it and got very serious. So I think in terms of dealing with the family, that was a tough scene. In terms of technical, the staging of the shark attack was very hard. It happened in six different locations including Oahu, Tahiti, and the Turtle Bay resort. So many different places! It was like a puzzle to put it all together, to make it look authentic. Shooting from helicopters and under water—it was just a huge challenge.

why do you think Bethany is an inspiration to so many people?

I think it's one of our greatest nightmares—the idea of being attacked by a shark. I know as a surfer, since *Jaws*, it spooked me. Then you take a 13-year-old girl who was attacked. It's beyond tragic. Most people would stop surfing. She went the opposite way. Not only does she surf, but she excels at it. It's a morality tale for us: life is going to give you ups and downs, but if you believe you can do it, nothing can stand in your way. Bethany is more than a survivor. She never allows anything or anyone to get in the way of her faith or her passion. She makes you believe anything is possible.

Lorraine Broussard Nicholson

Just the facts!

Birthdate: April 16, 1990

Famous folks: Daughter of actor Jack Nicholson and actress Rebecca Broussard

Hails from: Los Angeles, California

Her first role: Lorraine received her first film credit at the age of 13 in *Something's Gotta Give*, starring her dad, Diane Keaton, and Amanda Peet. It was a tiny walk-on part as a young girl in a market—but Lorraine was "bitten" by the acting bug!

Other credits: In 2004, Lorraine appeared in *The Princess Diaries 2: Royal Engagement* as Princess Lorraine, and played one of Adam Sandler and Kate Beckinsale's daughters in the 2006 movie *Click*. In 2007, she took her first leading role in the animated feature *Fly Me to the Moon*.

The envelope please . . . : Lorraine was Miss Golden Globe at the 64th Annual Golden Globes, handing out awards to all the winners!

playing Alana: Q&A with Lorraine Nicholson

what drew you to this project? what about the story spoke to you?

I remember when the news of Bethany's accident first hit the news circuit. I was eating breakfast before going off to school. My brother is terrified of sharks, so my mom tried to switch the channel. But I was entranced. Bethany was going to get back on the horse, as they say. Subconsciously, I think, her story continued to inspire me ever since that moment over pancakes. When they asked me to join the project, I was elated. I felt that the movie would help spread her message of hope and resiliency, and I wanted to be a part of it.

what was your first reaction to meeting Bethany? what surprised you about her? how would you describe her?

First reaction: she's so tall! After getting to know her for about thirteen seconds, I realized she was tough, too. Bethany's achievements are not simply a miracle. She works hard to achieve her goals! She expected the same out of everyone involved in the project, which is why we were all able to fulfill our greatest potentials. At the same time, she is the most open-minded, laid-back girl. Never, for a moment, does she judge anyone. Bethany pushes us all to be the best version of ourselves.

describe your character Alana. What motivates her?

A lot of my character drew its inspiration from the real Alana herself. After meeting her, I learned that despite her laid-back exterior, she is really insightful and funny. Alana is a professional athlete.

She has the drive to keep up with her fellow athletes. I wanted to incorporate this side of her as well as her more goofy, laid-back side. Alana and Bethany are lifelong friends. In the end, I wanted to make this aspect clear through my scenes with AnnaSophia.

did you get to know Bethany and the Hamilton family? spend time with them? what did you learn from them?

The Hamilton family was very involved with the movie and its process from start to finish. I spent a lot of time with them on set, sometimes goofing around, sometimes keeping it strictly business. On the day we shot the shark scene on the reef, it was very physically grueling. Caught in both the physical and emotional aspects, I dropped all my boundaries and cried hysterically throughout the scene. Little did I know, Mr. and Mrs. Hamilton were onshore, listening to the scene taking place. When I got back to shore, they seemed to be very emotionally affected. Overall, however, they were concerned about me, as I too was still feeling very emotional. I remember Cheri gave me the most glorious hug. It was a really fantastic moment for me, because I felt that I did them proud.

what do you find most inspiring about Soul Surfer? what is the message you hope moviegoers take away?

For me, Bethany's resiliency transcends all denominations of faith. For each of us, we face moments in our lives, like Bethany, that challenge all we believe in. We can either transcend these obstacles or turn our back on our true selves. Bethany shows us just what human beings are capable of. She is an inspiration to me, and I am thrilled to be involved in her life and story.

what is your favorite scene in the movie and why?

My favorite scene in the movie is definitely Bethany's Thanksgiving surf. She faces her fears, gets back on the board, and succeeds! Even shooting this scene, I got goose bumps.

what did you personally learn in making this movie (i.e., how to surf; about faith, etc.)?

I learned so much while shooting *Soul Surfer*. First, I learned how to cook, as I was living by myself for the first time without a school cafeteria! I made many delicious meals for all of my movie friends. Second, I learned how to surf. This was huge! At first, I felt that my arms were going to die, but eventually I was able to reach my goals and now I have the pleasure of being able to surf whenever I want! It's always fun to learn new skills. Lastly, by meeting Bethany, I learned what a person is capable of with a lot of hard work and faith in oneself.